RESPONSIBLE REVOLUTION

RESPONSIBLE REVOLUTION

Means and Ends
for Transforming Society

by Johannes Verkuyl
and
H. G. Schulte Nordholt

translated and edited by Lewis Smedes

WILLIAM B. EERDMANS PUBLISHING COMPANY

Grand Rapids, Michigan

Copyright © 1974 by William B. Eerdmans Publishing Company
All rights reserved

Printed in the United States of America

Translated from the second Dutch edition, *Verantwoorde
Revolutie,* © 1970, J. H. Kok N.V., Kampen

Library of Congress Cataloging in Publication Data

Verkuyl, Johannes.
 Responsible revolution.

 Translation of Verantwoorde revolutie.
 1. Revolution (Theology). 2. Revolution.
I. Schulte Nordholt, H. G.   II. Title.
BT738.3.V413   261.8'3   73-13560
ISBN 0-8028-1546-4

Contents

PART 1

REVOLUTION
The Response of Faith

by

JOHANNES VERKUYL

INTRODUCTION

In our day, everything that happens on the horizon of history is thrown upon a radar screen for all to see. Mass media give every man his own radar station on the world; all the movements of men on this planet happen before his eyes. And just as men on the bridge of a ship are summoned by what they see on radar to make decisions as to the course of the ship, we too have to ask ourselves what the things we see indicate as to the course we should follow.

We are gradually developing a global sense of responsibility. We are involved by everything that God puts on the agenda of today's world developments. He calls us to take notice of what is happening. He expects us to be concerned in a way that involves us in co-responsibility and, sometimes, guilt. It is not hard, if we keep our eyes open, to read the most important events that show up in the radar station of our diminishing world, and to discern priorities on God's agenda by the blips on the radar screen of mass media.

We will mention just a few.

The relationship between the rich and the poor countries does not and may not give us a single day's ease. We experience the flood of expectations in the poor countries and we feel the ebb tide of disappointment for millions who have waited in vain for justice, prosperity, and freedom. We are involved—whether we approve or not—in the struggle for social, economic, and political righteousness in worldwide perspective. God has put the question of the rich vs. poor countries on the agenda, and He calls for an answer.

Another item on the agenda of today is the relationship between races. Every day the tensions between the races are felt somewhere in the world, in Amsterdam and Chicago, in the mines of Johannesburg and in Lagos. The symptoms of racism, black, white, brown, or yellow racism, are present everywhere. This question, too, is high on God's agenda, and He wills that we attend to it. Antoher matter is that of war and peace in the atomic age. We all feel that this question has top priority, allowing for no postponement.

These are just a few matters that touch everyone, and illustrate how developments in the whole world are as close to everyone as one's TV set.

Anyone who pauses to think about developments in our world can see that development itself is a challenge. The situation cannot remain on dead center. And we cannot go back to better times of former centuries. We have no choice; we must keep moving. And for this reason, we must accept responsibility for the direction. We are called to think, to act, to help decide the course, to exert influence on the decisions that will shape the course of events in today's world.

The challenge of our time is thrown out to politicians, to economists, to sociologists, to anthropologists, to technologists, and to industrialists—to all those whose job it is to take leadership. But it comes also to any who can contribute his insights and his knowledge. The challenge is set at the doorsteps of theologians and at the chancel of the churches.

"The burning issues of our time form a challenge to the Christian churches, and to theology. What is needed now is Christian imagination to grasp the moral imperatives for effective actions to meet human need in worldwide dimensions. Our credibility and our obedience to the message of God's love for men in Jesus Christ, as well as the fundamental convictions of our faith respecting the being and destiny of men, are being tested by our answer to this challenge."

The above quotation is from the executive committee of the World Council of Churches meeting in Crete. But it was the Conference on Church and Society, held in Geneva in 1966, that set this challenge under the rubric of "a theology of revolution," or what others called a "theology of development" and what, it seems to me, can best be called "a theology of transformation."

This little book is an effort to put together the ingredients out of which theology and the church may be able to answer this challenge. We will not be focusing on concrete alternatives of action on the specific points of the agenda that haunts the world today. Each of these demands its own particular approach and its own particular response. I have tried to speak to specific points in other books. But here we will limit ourselves, in an introductory way, to general considerations.

THE BOOK OF LIBERATION

The Bible is a book that forever eludes our mastery. No single person, no single theologian, no single church, and no single century has ever captured the whole of it and made an end to further discovery within it. We are only small fruit-gatherers; we are never lords of this vineyard. This is why, over and over again, as times change, new and different perspectives from the Bible take hold of us and speak to us in wonderful new ways.

During the war, and while a prisoner, I was sometimes overwhelmed by biblical perspectives that came on me as a shining light in my prison cell, during days of hunger and utter misery, perspectives that never occurred to me in days of freedom. In our present time, in which we have a sense of being pushed headlong toward a new future, a time in which the peoples of the world appear to be setting out on a long march, toward who knows what destiny, a time in which more humane relations are groped for amid all sorts of inhuman situations, in our time, I say, still other biblical perspectives speak to us from this inexhaustible book, and now promise to become a *new* floodlight for the path that we, with the whole world, will have to follow.

Theologians offer their help to us in our digesting of these perspectives, and the literature in our hands is enormous. But I am not interested now in combing the field of theological works. I merely want to select a few biblical perspectives that strike me as of special meaning to us as we seek out a theology of transformation, a theology that will help us answer the challenge of our times and provide us spiritual strength on our way into the future.

1. Jahweh the Slave Liberator

The study of the environment in which the Old Testament was written, and the comparison of the living God of Israel with the Baalim of the neighbors of Israel, throws ever clearer light on what makes Israel's God, and faith in Him, truly unique. The Baalim, nature-gods, were the gods of the status quo. Jahweh is the God of the exodus, the God of liberation.

The cult objects of the Near East were bound to the cycle of the seasons. Faith in those gods robbed history of its meaning by denying the possibility of real change in history. But the God to whom the Old Testament witnesses is not the god of the status quo. He is the God who works and accomplishes new things through historical events. Israel believed that the God who made the sun, moon, and stars speaks to people in historical happenings. He is the God who rejects the status quo as a norm, leads Israel out of economic, political, and spiritual slavery, and goes on ahead of His people toward their new future.

The keyword in the Old Testament is: "I am Jahweh, your God, who led you out of the land of Egypt, out of the house of bondage" (Exodus 20:1). With this, the living God introduces Himself as the liberator of the slaves. He appears in human history and stakes everything on transforming a slave people into a nation of free men and women of God. Only after this powerful self-introduction of the God of Israel does the first command get heard: "You shall have no other gods before me" (Exodus 20:3).

Any "God" who does not act in history, who does not free slaves, whose chief concern is not to liberate men for authentic human life, who is not leading things along toward a kingdom in which God and his people live together, is not God at all but only a helpless idol.

2. The Meaning of Theocracy

Jahweh, the slave liberator, who frees His people from the pharaoh's structures of oppression, makes clear what His intentions are in the giving of the law and the formation of the theocracy. He intends to form a people that will live out His mercy and righteousness, a people who may in all their human relations give concrete shape and form to God's mercy and righteousness. God intends a fellowship in which God is God and people are real people, in which God and men live together in an unbreakable covenant of righteousness and love. This is theocracy. It failed continually in Israel's history. Indeed, it was meant only as a tentative signal among the nations to attract attention to God's bigger plan, one that touched not only Israel but all the nations of the world.

The God of the exodus, the God who leads the march to freedom, keeps going through history. He does not stop until the goal is reached and the Kingdom is realized, the Kingdom in which righteousness covers and permeates the whole of life.

3. The Prophets' Attack on Social Injustice

The prophets' task was to recall the real purpose God had for His people. When Israel sells its firstborn, when it practices injustice instead of serving righteousness, when it deals unfairly instead of being merciful, when it treats people inhumanely, then God sends His prophets with a measuring rod to take the measure of the individual and collective life, the personal relations and the social structures of Israel. The measuring rod is the law of Jahweh.

In Uppsala, a group of students produced a play by Alan Hartman, "On That Day," and presented it to the delegates at the 1968 World Council Assembly. The prophet Amos was the central figure of the play. He came on in startlingly modern dress. With his plumb line in his hand (Amos 7:7-9), he put God's measure to the life of individuals, of governments and nations, and measured the institutions and structures of the modern world against the demands of God's mercy and justice. This is the constant relevance of the prophets of Israel: they remind us of the purposes God has for people's lives, their social institutions and structures.

This is the core of everything they have to say to us: "He has made known to you, O man, what is good and what the Lord asks of you: to do justice, to love mercy, and to walk humbly with your God" (Micah 6:8).

4. *The Messianic King and the Coming of His Kingdom*

The Old Testament is a book of promise, and it is a book of messianic homesickness. The New Testament is the book of the Kingdom, already come and still to come. In Jesus Christ the new Kingdom arrived, the Kingdom God had set his heart on. The coming of Jesus settles it. He is the salvation that has come, wholly here, on earth. In His person and work the Kingdom of God came to pass.

In Jesus' life, through His death on the cross, in His resurrection from death, God was taking hold of the powers that held us slaves; and so it happened that reconciliation came about, that sins were forgiven. The liberating action was done, and the foundation of a new world was laid.

The miracles Jesus did were flashes of light that signalled the arrival of the Kingdom. Sick people were healed. Dead people were raised. Blind men saw again. Hopeless people found hope. Possessed men were given relief. Lonely ones found fellowship. And the poor and the prisoners heard the bells ring out freedom.

But the New Testament, too, is a book of promise. It was in the midst of life still unredeemed, in the midst of the world where Jesus was hanged on a cross, that God's Kingdom began. The Kingdom has come, but it is still to come. Salvation is present and is still to be revealed. It is finished, and it will be finished on another day.

The parables of Jesus are hints of how God is bridging the distance between the "already" and the "not yet" of the Kingdom. From the beginning moments of the Kingdom to its final revelation, God uses methods that suit Him and the nature of His Kingdom. They are the methods of the seed, of the fishnet, of the yeast, of handing out talents and responsibilities, of the lamps that must be kept burning through the night—these, all of them and each of them, are clues to God's methods.

The New Testament says quite clearly that the beginning is not the same as the ending, and that the final and glorious revelation is still on its way. But Christ, who is and was and is still to come, is our hope in the meanwhile. The last revelation of the Kingdom of justice and peace is coming. The last word is not the word of hate, or injustice, of faithlessness, or of inhumanity. The last word is justice, because the last word belongs to Him on whom our hope is set. The perfect redemption is still waiting.

But the Redeemer lives and He is on His way. He goes ahead. He is working out His program. He is already the Victor, and He is seeing to the end of His struggle against all unrighteousness, hard-heartedness, and inhumanity. Meanwhile, He wants to involve us too in His struggle, right here, in our time and place in history.

5. The Expectation of the Kingdom: What It Means Now

Everything that the Bible says to us about the Kingdom that has come and is coming still, everything about the Lord's way of taking us into the van of His coming, can be summed up in one sentence from II Peter.

"We look forward, according to His promise, to a new heaven and a new earth wherein justice dwells" (II Peter 3:13).

This is the sentence that distills the essence of biblical hope. In this powerful word we find everything that all the prophets and the apostles had to say about the future that is centered on Him who is and is still to come.

The "home of justice," the New English Bible has it. Not some hit-and-miss improvements in human relations, not some spotty token justice brought in here or there. We expect an earth where justice is global, final, and completely at home.

What this means is a new state of affairs, a new order in

which the relations between God and men, and among men, as well as between groups, are all set straight—and are experienced in festivity. The new will be a place of celebration. The fellowship between God and man, and the righteousness between men—all the way, involving racial, social, economic, cultural, and political spheres—will be carried on in a mood of perpetual holiday.

We must not shrink our expectations, or be puny-minded about God's promises. Christians sometimes suppose that God will be satisfied to have us in heaven, with just a single wing of the cosmic house renewed. This is small-minded thinking, because God will not rest until the whole of the cosmos is restored.

Moreover, it is important to remember that this promise does more than crystallize the valid expectations of the prophets, the apostles, and the whole Christian church. It congeals the mandate that the promise implies for human relationships here and now: it tells us how, in view of our expectations for the future, we should manage our lives and our affairs in the present.

The expectation of a new heaven and new earth has now and then aroused in those who do not share it a rebuke against the expecters: those who hope, it is claimed, show little awareness that their hope involves a summons to shape life now after the pattern of the hope. "Religion—opiate of the people." "Pie in the sky." "Christians too busy with heaven to be responsible for the earth." And so forth. These are stereotyped criticisms levelled against the Christian hope, judgments that were especially common at the turn of the last century. To people outside the Christian community, the promised hope had the trappings of egotistic, soft romanticism that had little awareness of the need for hard justice among men on earth.

James Baldwin, speaking at the Uppsala meetings of the World Council of Churches (1968), indicted Christians for hoarding the gospel like uninvested capital instead of using it as the power of God that can renew the structures of our social life. There is, I think, a shameful basis for his stinging complaint. But nothing could be more contrary to the spirit of the prophets and apostles than to ignore the implications of our future hope for the nagging problems of the here and now.

Just before Peter focused our hope on the new heavens and new earth, he said: "Think what sort of people you ought to be, what devout and dedicated lives you should live! Eagerly await the coming of the Day of God and work to hasten it on" (II Peter 3:11, 12). Two phrases stand out here as indicators of what our posture should be: "Eagerly await" and "work to hasten."

Christoph Blumhardt (b. 1842) was among the first to let these words form the starting point for his vision of the future. He let his whole life's orientation center on the coming of Christ and His Kingdom, the gracious rule of God over all the earth. Karl Barth wrote of Blumhardt: "The prophetic dimension of Blumhardt's message and apostolate lay in this, that the expecting and hastening, the present and the yet to be, met each other, joined and completed each other, in all his talk and all his action" (*Klärung und Wirkung,* 1966, p. 289).

Thousands of people were turned on by his restlessness, moved by what moved him, gripped both by what gave him rest and by what drove him to feverish activity. Our point here is not to talk about Blumhardt; it is only to use his memory as a way of underlining one thing: our hope for a new earth must move us both to "eagerly await" and to "work to hasten" the day.

If we look forward only to death, we may just as well say: "Come, let us eat and drink, for tomorrow we shall die." Or, "let injustice run free, for the brutal shall inherit half the earth." If one builds his expectations on human potential or on specific social and political systems, he is likely to be disenchanted, disillusioned; he may turn his enthusiasm into cynicism and desperation. The nonconformist of today becomes the conformist of tomorrow—if he stakes everything on what men can do. People who are full of hope today—if their hopes rest on men—are empty of it the next day. Today's progressives become tomorrow's conservatives. But he who looks forward to the future of Jesus Christ learns to "wait" and "work to hasten."

Wait: we are not going to blow soap bubbles or build castles of sand.

We are not going to confuse the ecumenical movement with the New Jerusalem—we wait. We are not going to identify the United Nations with the promise of a new earth—we wait. We are not going to pin our hopes on the results of social and economic development, certainly not on any political breakthrough, as though they might be the harbinger of the promised time when justice shall reign—we wait.

But we also *work to hasten.* This means that we see to it that injustice is put down and that justice wins out. It means that, believing, we strive to erect *signs* and to *discover* signs that the new earth is indeed coming.

"Work to hasten"—this means that we create parables, set up experimental illustrations and test models of what we still expect to come. To wait without "working to hasten" is to sit still with arms folded. It is to turn faith into an easy chair. It is to become a spiritual groundhog that does not invest a dime in his environment. This is an unbiblical posture. It is not even a genuine attitude, it is sheer negation. To "work to hasten" without accepting the reality of waiting is to become an activist quickly drained of the confidence and joyful certainty that Jesus Christ will make good on what He promises. But to wait *and* to work, to rest *and* to move, this is to live out of the promise of a new heaven and a new earth.

Consider a weight lifter. He lets his whole body relax and then concentrates it completely into the one job of lifting the weights. Rest and movement keep each other in balance. This is how it is with waiting *and* working with eyes peeled for the coming of the Lord. Resting in the promise and working to hasten are kept in balance.

Karl Barth wrote of Christoph Blumhardt: "His secret was the constant movement between waiting and hastening, between adventuresome involvement in the middle of the present time and a surprising inner turning toward what shall yet be done through the power from on high. This man, rooted in God, had a singularly living relation with his time, and neither war nor revolution could disillusion him" (*loc. cit.*).

What Barth said of Blumhardt ought to be the spirit of anyone who both "awaits" and "works to hasten" the new earth. He does not suffer from sickly illusions. He is not turned into a cynic or defeatist when the dreams do not come true. He knows he has to keep on awaiting what is not yet here while he works to hasten its coming. And what he waits for is nothing short of a new earth in which justice takes over the whole of human life.

2

THEOLOGY'S WORD
TO REVOLUTIONARY TIMES

The times call for a theology of transformation. In the previous chapter we listed some aspects of a biblical perspective that could provide the impulse for a theology of transformation. In this chapter we want to review how the church and theology have in fact responded and, in some cases, still respond to the challenges of the times with a theology and practice of counterrevolution. Along with a theology of antirevolution, they have offered a theology of the status quo. Further, we can distinguish a pietistic response which, with a polite bow, has simply side-stepped the questions and challenges of its day.

1. The Theology of Counterrevolution

The church and its theology have often responded to the urgings to reform the power and economic structures of society by defending the old system and resisting any and all efforts to renew society.

At the Conference on Church and Society in Geneva (1966), the Russian Archbishop Vitaly Borovoi recalled the position a large section of the Russian Orthodox hierarchy took in response to the compelling need for a renewal of the structures of Czarist society. He recalled how the Byzantiumcontrolled Russian Orthodox church preferred to camouflage the flagrant injustices in the existing order and how, rather than search for alternatives to the rising tide of Leninism, the church supported all direct measures brought *against* any change. Thus it lost millions of members and bargained away its credibility among the masses. Without denying the ideological and practical tensions that the Russian church currently experiences, Borovoi pressed the point that the church and its theology cannot afford to take the stance of counterrevolution in prerevolutionary, revolutionary, or postrevolutionary times.

China affords us another example of a counterrevolutionary church. It was particularly the Roman Catholic Church, by means of its so-called Mary-legions, that pushed counterrevolution during the most corrupt period of the Kuomintang and in the early period of the rise of Maoism. Instead of seeking alternatives, it followed the line of counterrevolution. Johannes Schütte's impressive book, *Die Katholischen Mission im Spiegel der rotchinesischen Presse* (1956) is a kind of penance for Catholic mistakes, without lapsing into self-flagellation and without whitewashing the communist regime's hostile policy toward the churches in present-day China.

The Portuguese church leaders, thankfully only in part, were crassly counterrevolutionary in Angola and Mozambique. This is also true of the church in pre-Castro Cuba.

Leslie Dewart, the Roman Catholic theologian from Toronto, wrote a chapter called "The Theology of Counter-revolution" in his book, *Christianity and Revolution* (1968). There he analyzes statements made by the Archbishop of Cuba, Perez Serantes, while Castro was just beginning his attack against the Batista regime, a time when it was still possible to have led Cuba in socialistic rather than communist paths. The archbishop gave lip service to the fairly progressive papal encyclicals, *Quadragesimo anno* and *Rerum novarum*. But these encyclicals were mere museum pieces in Cuba, since not a step was ever taken to practice what they taught. The words were fine, but they signalled nothing more. Moreover, his statements were defenses of the old feudal-hierarchical social structure without a hint of understanding that these structures created and sustained systematic injustice.

The United States, according to Dewart, failed to grasp that what was going on in Cuba was not just another palace coup native to South America. The American administration did not seem to comprehend, until late in the day, that the whole structure of Cuban society was in process of radical change. They did not understand, claims Dewart, because the interests of American investors—interests that, in the Cuban economy, played the role of robber barons by the grace of Batista—blinded it to the facts. The United States then broke off all relations with Cuba and, by that decision, forced Cuba into dependence on Russia. It was in this situation that the archbishop compared the choice between Washington and Moscow with a choice between Christ and anti-Christ, and urged the Cuban people to make a "wise" choice. The archbishop showed little trace of humility, gave little hint of insight into the unrighteousness of the old order; he was blind and deaf to the signs of the times.

I have no desire to laud the present regime in Cuba. It is an extreme leftist dictatorship. Any criticism of the regime from within is regarded as counterrevolutionary. Dissenters have either fled or are in jail, including socialist critics. The young are thoroughly indoctrinated. It is a totalitarian, communist regime. Cuba, however, is a reality in the Caribbean, as China is in Asia, and has to be accepted as such. Only an internal reformation to bring about greater humanization in Cuba will successfully change the situation there. But as we shake our heads at the totalitarian dimensions of Cuban life, let us remember that at one time the Roman Catholic Church had the chance to inspire a transformation of the old order and would not, choosing instead to pursue a theology and practice of counter-revolution. Churches outside Cuba ought now to support, as best they can, those courageous Roman Catholics and Protestants who have stayed there and are seeking ways of penitence and renewal in Cuban life.

These are just a few reminders of the church's counterrevolutionary policy during times when a policy of transformation might have changed the course of history. There are more, for example the church in South America, which is pushing its theology of counterrevolution as consistently as any church ever has.

He who has ears to hear, let him hear what the Spirit is teaching through the history of churches whose theology is counterrevolutionary.

2. Theology of Restoration

a. Natural Law as a Model of Restoration Theology

Theology's answer to the challenge of ongoing transformation has been, too often, the doctrine of natural law. Since natural-law theologians do realize that societies need reformation, we can call their thinking restoration theology. The background of natural law is too well known to need discussion here. What is worth noting is that even in these times of profound change and radical challenges, the theology of restoration is still being applied.

Roman Catholic theology has through the centuries defended the existing orders, and sought somehow to preserve intact the bond between throne and altar. On the one hand, Catholic theology since Vatican II has shown promising signs of creating a theology of renewal, and has critically, flexibly, and dynamically sought to point a way into the future with the biblical motif of the coming Kingdom of God. On the other hand, Catholic theologians are still trying to find their way along the path of natural law and natural theology. The encyclical *Progressio populorum* is an example of the first tendency, while *Humanae vitae* is an example of the second.

Latin America is the scene of both Catholic approaches. On the one hand we see a dynamic figure like Dom Helder Camara, a sort of modern Moses who has dared to say No to the pharaohs of the military junta. And on the other, we have the prelates who give the impression that they are living in the days of Pope Gregory XVI and Pius XII, and who still lend their authority to sacralize the persistent feudal-hierarchical structures.

There are progressive bishops in Latin America who are

trying to provide leadership in the effort to find ways of renewal in society. But these are a small minority. The overwhelming majority are content, like paladins of a Spanish Christendom, to stand watch over the status quo. They are content with a theology of restoration that cannot possibly provide a genuine architectonic critique of the disorderly order of today's society.

  b. The Doctrine of the Two Kingdoms as a Model of Restoration Theology

Martin Luther's notion of the two kingdoms is well known. He spoke of the kingdom of the right and the kingdom of the left, God's rule in the area of history and God's rule in the arena of the gospel. The secular domain was arranged through divine laws which penetrated the world from the very beginning and managed to keep the divine orders intact within the history of fallen man. These orders were given for the support and formation of human life in marriage, family, society, and governments. There are no revealed forms or concrete rules for the maintenance of the orders. These are developed and reformed in history by means of human reason in response to the fundamental mandate given to man. They are open to the possibility that they can be misused and distorted in human ideas and ideologies. In principle, the orders are preserved by law, and we must not intrude such qualities as love, or faith, or sin within this arena. God rules in the territory of law whether the persons involved happen to know Him or not.

Alongside the secular order stands the spiritual order, or the eschatological Kingdom of Christ. Here eternal salvation is offered, freedom from sin, the devil, and death. The means used in this kingdom are faith and love.

The two kingdoms are mixed only at great cost, according to Luther. They should not be confused, nor should they be joined. God rules in each kingdom in ways and means that fit each and not the other.

Luther's ideas on this matter have been gone over with a fine comb by hundreds of scholars. But the interpretation of Luther's doctrine is of great historical importance. My view is that Luther showed clear signs of favoring restoration theology in regard to social and political questions. It led to a division between personal and churchly life on one side and political and social activities on the other. The seriousness of the social situation did not register much with him, and he all too easily branded as a fanatic anyone who tried to put society to the touchstone of the gospel.

Luther's doctrine has always tended to favor the conservative elements, and is always used as a theological basis for alliances between throne and altar. It fostered, in later times, the notion of an all but absolute separation between personal morality and official morality. The morality of the Sermon on the Mount applies to the personal and inner life of individuals. Official morality applies to the ordering of state and society, including the functions of government. This dichotomy went hand in hand with a glorification of the sword. Friedrich Naumann once remarked that he was obliged by the pulpit not to covet anything that was his neighbor's, but that as a member of the government he was called to obey the law: "Thou shalt covet the Bosporus and the Dardanelles." This is typical of the sort of division of territory that the Lutheran two-kingdom doctrine inspired in later German Lutheranism.

Under the influence of romanticism and idealism, Reinhold Seeberg (*Christian Ethics,* 1911) and Friedrich Brunstäd tried to take the two-kingdom doctrine in new directions. Rather than leaving the relation between the Kingdom of God and the kingdom of the world up to individual decisions, they claimed that the forces that determined the development of society were rooted in creation. National socialism tried to annex this interpretation of the two-kingdom doctrine to support its own absolutistic regime. That a large segment of German Lutheranism went along with this shows not only how dreadfully malformed the two-kingdom doctrine had become, but also that the original doctrine carried stirrups by which the ideology of national socialism could be brought into the saddle. Bonhoeffer was one of the few who unmasked the deception and protested against it at the cost of his life.

After the war, men like H. D. Wendland and Ernst Wolff

wrestled with the distortions of the two-kingdom notion and tried to come up with a new interpretation of it. Wolff, for instance, concluded that the struggle for civil justice is laid on the man who is justified by faith. But the traditional teaching of the two kingdoms is still dominant, as is clear in the declarations of the bishops of the "Landeskirchen." In fact, it is being flown on banners to the accompaniment of the beating of theological drums. H. O. Wölber, then bishop of Hamburg, flew the banner when he sabotaged the efforts of the Evangelical Church in West Germany to translate the need for reconciliation into political terms in relations with Poland. The bishop of Kurhessen, worried that the church might forfeit the state's support, summoned the two-kingdom doctrine to urge the churches to refrain from making any political declarations. In *Christen Democratische Union* circles there is considerable maneuvering to see to it that the two-kingdom doctrine is respected by the churches. Thus the doctrine is still used to take the comfort and sting out of the promises and demands of God whenever they touch anything within the terrain of the worldly orders.

Dutch Lutheran C. W. Mönnich wrote recently: "The doctrine of the two kingdoms can function in certain historical contexts, where there is a Christian society, even when it is being threatened, and in which the government might be viewed as the preserver of God's order in civil affairs. But it is my judgment that this doctrine, when it is shoved on us from the outside as is happening in Germany today, can bring disastrous consequences." Mönnich is absolutely right in my opinion. It would be better to scrap the whole doctrine and to abandon efforts to give it new form for our day.

I was strengthened in this conviction by a trip through South Africa. There a Lutheran theologian, E. A. Ludemann, has tried to weigh the statements of the Council of Churches in South Africa in the scale of the two-kingdom doctrine. The result again is to negate all efforts to speak to South Africa's critical social situation from the perspective of God's promises and demands. Criticisms are shoved aside in the name of the two-kingdom doctrine and the church is left with nothing to say to the established structures of society. A vigorous effort to preserve a status quo theology is made by churchmen in a situation that needs evaluation in the light of God's law and God's gospel much more than it needs the support of Lutheran confessions.

c. The Doctrine of Creation Ordinances as a Model of Restoration Theology

The doctrine of creation ordinances still influences the Anti-Revolutionary Party in the Netherlands, and tends to lead Christian political action in the direction of restoration rather than renewal.

Groen van Prinsterer, father of Protestant politics in the Netherlands, used a slogan: "It is written. It is historical." He tended to view the past historical development of social orders and structures as normative. And since they were themselves norms, they were not tested by the biblical norms. Abraham Kuyper also used the notion of creation ordinances, and worked his theory out in his famous, *Ons Program* (Our Program). J. J. Buskes wrote: "In original Calvinism, the 'It is written' was dynamite beneath the 'It is historical.' But since Groen van Prinsterer it has been different. Historical achievements tend to become normative, while historical distortion is not taken seriously" ("De Sociale Kracht van het Calvinisme," in *De Maatschappij van Nu en Morgen,* 1948, p. 213).

Karl Barth's objection to the creation ordinance idea is directed mostly at Emil Brunner, but he also includes Groen's ideas in his criticism: "We can honor the Lord of history only *in* the Lord of the Holy Scriptures and the Lord of the Church. While in the midst of world history with all its distorted situations and structures, we ought to listen to the Word of God and learn to be obedient to Christ."

It would be inaccurate to argue that Abraham Kuyper's political ideas were wholly based on a doctrine of creation ordinances à la Groen van Prinsterer. He was much more willing than Groen to address criticism against society. A striking example is found in his famous address to the first Christian-social congress, published in America as *Christianity and the Class Struggle* (1950). It must also be said to the lasting honor of Kuyper that he was first among his countrymen to reject the colonial structure and to make its liquidation a priority for his Christian political program. But it is undeniable that many of Kuyper's ideas were expressions of a theology of restoration and the status quo: his thoughts on race questions, the relationship between cultures, the problem of the division of powers and wealth are stamped more by conservatism and romanticism than by evangelical depth.

Dr. O. Noordmans, in a debate with Klaas Schilder that was carried in *De Reformatie* (January 1936—the year is significant), cited a number of quotations from Kuyper's *Gemeene Gratie* (*Common Grace*). There we hear Kuyper speaking of the "Northern dynamic for life" over against the "unproductive South" (Vol. I, p. 368), of the Europeans as "the best race" (II, p. 670), and mingled in among such statements, now and then a hint of anti-Semitism (I, p. 382).

Noordmans comments: "To speak about a 'best race' in Northern Europe, and to betray strong suggestions of anti-Semitism, requires of any theologian an accounting of the political faith nestled in such statements. There is here a strange notion that grace works through biological processes, and we know where such notions can lead. One cannot make use of notions like this and remain innocent. The lightning of history has flashed, and has made straddling the fence even more illegitimate than it was at Mt. Carmel in Elijah's day."

This was a prophetic utterance in 1936. And it is worth thinking about, because the same doctrine of creation ordinances that led Kuyper to the strange expressions we have noted is being used today by some theologians in the churches in South Africa. It is argued that the segregated development of races is tied to the ordinances of creation and must be respected forever. In actuality, this pseudo-biblical ideology is dedicated to perpetuate the status quo of a system of political and economic exploitation. It is to be hoped that we shall not have to wait for the lightning of history to strike in South Africa, but that efforts of courageous church leaders to release South African life from this pseudo-biblical ideology may prosper and that life there may yet be renewed in response to the gospel.

It is ironic that a prophetic critic like Kuyper should be vulnerable to exploitation by South African theologians to support their racial ideology. The Anti-Revolutionary Party is burdened by the theology of ordinances in much the same way as the Catholic party is by the doctrine of natural law. Christian radicalism is therefore legitimate in this situation, because it can humbly and honestly play a critical role over against a theology that too seldom brings the existing order under the judgment of God's law and gospel.

The challenges of our time cannot be answered with a restoration theology, or a theology of the status quo. Theologies of restoration and of counterrevolution have always aroused the judgment of men like Voltaire and Karl Marx, Goya and Brecht, who have charged that they use the "vertical dimension" to sabotage necessary criticism of social injustices. Theologies of the status quo, they claimed, manipulate the "eternal" as a bulwark against progress and as a foundation for castles of conservatism. Truth and falsehood are mingled in this judgment, but it does offer enough truth for all Christians to listen to it well and accept it humbly.

During the last morning devotional period at Uppsala, Elisabeth Adler of Berlin offered this prayer: "Lord, we have made your love, your righteousness, and your peace problematic in our world. We have supported systems of injustice, and have even tried to justify them with our theology. We have spoken softly to the powerful of the world and left the poor to their fate. We have preached peace and would not let our hands get dirty in political affairs. We have made half-baked resolutions against war, against economic injustice, against racial discrimination, and have by our actions supported the status quo. In our life and acts we have followed the false gods of our world. Lord, forgive us." We were moved then to pray, and we are still moved to pray in this spirit.

3. Pietism: Avoiding the Questions

Pietism is found in the developing countries as it is in the richer lands. By pietism we mean an approach to man that concentrates on his private experience of faith and conversion. Negatively, we mean by pietism a tendency to soft-pedal the responsibility to do the will of God in the area of politics and social structures or, in short, to avoid the cultural mandate of the gospel. This pietistic impulse is in some churches a rivulet and in others the mainstream of life. Pietism is too concerned with the soul to be much bothered with the body and the brains. The pietist defends his stance by saying that he concentrates on spiritual matters in order to avoid wasting time and energy, of which there is limited supply, on matters of lesser importance. Only one thing is necessary—the salvation of souls.

I strongly believe that this individualist and spiritualist concentration is in conflict with the very gospel that pietism honors as central to life. It may be true that the powers of sin and demons dominate the terrain of politics, society, economics, and culture. But the Lord is Lord of all the earth, and of every man that lives in it; and no man therefore can live under the gospel and escape responsibility for social and political life on earth.

One of the contributions of pietism is the growth of vital fellowship among the followers of Jesus. But these fellowships tend in time to become closed communities based on certain taboos and styles that isolate them from the world. The positive influence of pietism comes from its stress on personal involvement with the Bible. But the regrettable side of this is that pietistic circles frequently believe that they possess the only true interpretation of the Bible, and that they see in the Bible only the lines that lead to the individual. Thus, they tend to lack awareness that the light of the Bible shines out over all the great questions of society.

Pietistic circles tend to avoid the social and political questions. They invite flight instead of struggle. They urge disengagement instead of engagement, resignation instead of exercise of responsibility in the world.

New Christian intellectuals in developing countries often complain that the Western missionary is too pietistic. A Christian nationalist in Indonesia, who had been a prisoner of the Japanese during the war, told me that he had discovered the book of Amos for the first time while he was in prison. He complained that the missionaries he had known had never explained Amos to him in a way that was relevant to the struggle against injustices in the colonial system. Later, naively and uncritically, he became involved with some communist leaders who convinced him that they had an analysis of the colonial situation, and a purpose and strategy for the areas of life that the churches had left unattended and unjudged.

An Indonesian general, Dr. Tahi Simatupang, wrote that in the rise of the Indonesian republic the churches failed to provide any leadership. It was, he wrote, only through his contacts with the World Council of Churches that he discovered that God's promises and demands had any real import for the totality of human life. Now he is a leading figure in the Indonesian Council of Churches, a Christian thinker and politician, and has made a vital contribution to Indonesian society.

Emilio Castro of Uruguay expressed the same complaint against pietism in Latin America as Luthuli and Z. K. Matthews did in South Africa.

Pietism, unconsciously for the most part, makes a private agreement with the powers of the world: "We will concentrate on the hereafter and the personal, and you may occupy the arena of political and social affairs." The powers promise in return: "We will support you as long as you limit yourself to the arena of the private spiritual life of individuals."

Billy Graham in *World Aflame* (1965) records President Johnson's irritation with theologians who thought themselves competent to declare themselves on the race question and on the unsavory topic of napalm bombs. Unfortunately, Graham has tended to share such feelings. But he forgets that since the day of Elijah the prophet, who stood before Ahab, since John the Baptist, who stood up against Herod, since John Huss, Dietrich Bonhoeffer, and Beyers Naude, the servants of the Lord (whose rule goes beyond the soul) have spoken the truth about political, economic, and racial injustice just as they have cared for the spirit. When they did, it cost them popularity, but it gave them a prophetic credibility lacking in those who speak powerfully to the soul while they keep silence on collective unrighteousness.

We may hope that representatives of pietism and representatives of those who seek to address the gospel to society can find each other, influence each other, and provide needed corrections of each other. They need one another. This is particularly true in the student world. To mention just one instance, students in the developing countries are experiencing tension between the Inter-Varsity Fellowship and the World Federation of Christian Students. Both of these groups need what the other has. The I.V.F. tends to ignore the horizontal dimension of Christian responsibility while it stresses the vertical. The W.F.C.S. tends to reverse the priorities. Communication between these groups is imperative.

Pietists have done immeasurably significant work in making the name of Jesus known among the nations of the world. What a blessing it will be if pietists around the world are truly grasped both by the Bible *and* history and recognize what the expected advent of the Lord means for the totality of life—that we are, under the Lord's gracious and triumphant leadership, on our way to a new heaven and a new earth where justice will prevail over the length and breadth of it.

What was said about the Inter-Varsity Fellowship and the World Federation of Christian Students applies equally to the conciliar churches and the "conservative evangelicals." Fruitful conversation between the World Council and the evangelical churches occurs far too seldom. The evangelicals need to bring their keen appreciation for personal piety into the conversation as they listen to the appeal that the gospel must be brought to bear upon social and political questions as well.

3

TOWARD A THEOLOGY
OF TRANSFORMATION

The phrase "theology of revolution" has been pretty well
relieved of inevitable misunderstanding since Richard Shaull
baptized it into theological jargon in his *Encounter with Revolution* (1955). So, my own preference for "theology of transformation" may need some explanation. I have personally
learned a great deal from the plethora of writings on the theology of revolution, and I also associate myself with many of
their ideas. But experience has taught me that the word revolution covers so much ground, and is open to so many negative images, that it is perhaps better to try another word. The
word revolution, for many, says violence; and real revolutions
are often violent. So a theology of revolution can be read too
easily as a theology for the justification of violence, whether
extreme leftist or extreme rightist.

An ideology of violence and violent revolution is on its way
to taking hold on men's minds these days, an ideology as
dangerous as any other. The theology of counterrevolution and
the status quo was influenced, consciously or unconsciously, by
an unchristian ideology that refuses to test the government use
of force by the standards of justice, love, and mercy, and instead demands blind obedience to everything the government
determines. (Authority is authority and a rebel is a rebel.)

In the same way, by reaction, some theology, influenced by the ideology of guerilla revolution, gives a priori legitimacy to the use of certain types of violence; if it is guerilla violence, no matter what its quality, purpose, or circumstances, it is good violence. The altars for this ideology are erected in many places, the processions before its gods can be seen on many city streets, and its fuzzy slogans confuse our perspectives and distort our judgments.

Worshippers of the status quo have no monopoly on inhumanity. People who blindly shout for the downfall of the establishment are infected with it as well. The ideology of revolution arouses armchair revolutionaries (revolutionaries who are careful not to dirty their own hands out on the street), who can be heard uttering such nonsense as that we need a few more Vietnams in the world. These cultic disciples of violent revolutions tend to forget that chaos is the worst enemy the poor and oppressed could wish for. They seem obtuse to the fact that violent revolutions have seldom brought about a genuinely better condition for the poor people, and in fact are for the most part a demonic impulse. Most violent revolutions, as Hannah Arendt says (*On Revolution,* 1963), have been morally indefensible. Bloody revolutions are usually mad adventures that lead to anarchy and sadistic aggressiveness. They exchange one group of scoundrels for another group of scoundrels. Instead of introducing a new era of justice, they give birth to anarchy. They can function as an alibi for sheer lust, murder, and brutal, generalized inhumanity. Despising the route of patient progress toward necessary reforms, men can be so intoxicated by the passion of revolution that they destroy what chances there are of real social achievements.

The suggestion, floating freely in much revolutionary talk, that the first and only way to transform society is the use of violence, must be refuted. Herbert Marcuse has injected this thought into several of his writings, and some others of his ilk go still further than he does. There are undeniably valid aspects to much of what Marcuse says, and we ought to take them seriously. For instance, he has clearly put today's technological developments to the touchstone of humanity, and done so with the clearest of perception. More clearly than most, he has exposed the regressions and enslavements that our society involves for many people. Marcuse must be heard carefully by anyone who is trying to understand developments in modern society. But especially in his later writings, Marcuse opts for the use of violence, and rejects nonviolence, in pursuit of the objectives of the New Left. After his widely read book *One-Dimensional Man* (1964), he went on in *A Critique of Pure Tolerance* (1968) to urge intolerance for the right and tolerance only for leftists, and to prescribe the use of violence in short and intense actions. The espousal of violence is worked out still further in his *Essay on Liberation* (1969).

In the rise of figures like Cohn-Bendit in France and Dutschke in West Germany, we have seen that the chain of violence and counterviolence is forged as violent acts create a polarization between extreme-right and extreme-left. The preoccupation with violence, the mood in which men are ready to adopt violence as the first and only way to change, threatens to spread like an epidemic over today's world. It is striking how the theories of men like Marcuse are almost exact reproductions of those of Georges Sorel, the French neo-Marxist whose *Reflections on Violence* (10th ed., 1946, Eng. ed. 1950) had such a strong hold on several extremist groups between the world wars. Remarkably, Sorel was really a syndicalistic Marxist; but both Stalinists and the Mussolini clique, leftist as well as rightist extremists, took inspiration from his plea for anti-parliamentary violence, and transformed the theories of this rather aloof aristocrat (who would never have dirtied his own hand in the real business of violence) into practices that later nauseated the world.

Against Sorel's theories during that period came the voice of Julien Benda. Responding to Sorel's ideas, Benda wrote a book on the betrayal of the intellectuals in which he exposed the armchair radicals' own unwillingness to do anything about the real problems; he powerfully expressed disgust for cheap intellectual connivance with violence, whether for the extreme right or left wing. We recall also the pure voice of Simone Weil, who sensed beforehand the explosion of violence and counterviolence to which the theories of the aristocratic rebels could lead.

Many of Marcuse's views are reminiscent of Sorel. It is true that, for a neo-Marxist and syndicalist like Sorel, violence takes on a more self-justifying function than it does for the neo-Marxist Marcuse. Still, Marcuse does proclaim the a priori morality of violence when used by the left, just as he denounces as immoral anything that resists leftist violence.

The glorification of violence travels fast around the world. The idolatry of Mao and his Little Red Book, the cultic hero-worship given to Castro and Che Guevara, form a romantic clustering for a new kind of Jacobin revolutionism. A kind of pseudo-messianic spirit is at work in it. There is something of an echo of the call to the crucified Christ: "Come down from the cross and we will believe in you."

The ideology of self-justifying violence is a serious threat. There are specimens of "theology of revolution" that are much more profoundly influenced by this ideology than they are by the demands of the gospel. "Guerilla theologies," to use Charles West's phrase, get us nowhere. They are naive as they are dangerous. In most theologies of revolution there is too little discriminating judgment given to means and ends in the process of renewal. There is little awareness of the deep difference between the spirit of Barabbas and the spirit of Jesus Christ in the renewal efforts. Sometimes it seems as though it makes no difference whether we follow Barabbas or Christ, whether we demand the blood of others or whether we are willing to shed our own blood should it come to the necessity of blood-shedding at all.

In Asia and Africa, I have noted, people are often offended at naive prattle about a theology of revolution and an ideology of violence. In these continents too many are living in a post-revolutionary world to be attracted to easy talk about justifying violence. They have had their fill of bloody revolutions. They have known firsthand how full of demonic temptations bloody revolutions are. Fuzzy utopianism is not likely to hyp-notize them. They experience day by day that the real prob-lems just begin when men awaken from their revolutionary ecstasy and put their hands to the tools of building again. They have lived through the discovery that an exchange of a new regime for an old one offers no guarantees that the new regime will misuse its powers any less than did the old. One need only recall the situations of Nigeria and Indonesia, or those in Cuba, China, and Czechoslovakia. The Christians of Latin America who live in a prerevolutionary era and are hungry for change are not eager to take the route of violence as the first and only way to renewal. The armchair revolutionaries would do well to listen to them.

So, to avoid misunderstanding, I have chosen to use the phrase: theology of transformation.

Others opt for other ways of saying it. Simatupang speaks of a "theology of the modernization of traditional societies." Kenneth Cragg uses the phrase "theology of development." Jürgen Moltmann has made "theology of hope" a sign of our times. Rubem Alves of Brazil calls it "a theology of human hope." I am borrowing "theology of transformation" from Emilio Castro of Uruguay for both historical and theological reasons.

The phrase has a background in the Reformation adage *Ecclesia Reformata semper reformanda* (the Reformed Church must keep on being reformed). But Reformers like Calvin, Knox, Comenius, and others, also claimed another adage: *Societas semper reformanda* (society must be continually reformed). They were committed to a theology of transformation based on their vision of the promises and demands of God. It seems to me that we will do well to keep their vision alive in our time.

But there is a biblical and theological reason for preferring the phrase "theology of transformation." The biblical message is one neither of evolution nor of revolution. It is a message of transformation, of change, of renewal. We are not urging a departure into virgin territory when we ask for a theology that recognizes the social and political structures of life as a legitimate theological concern. Much to the contrary. A large number of theologians, in the North as well as the South, have been and are vigorously involved in the development of a theology of renewal. Some of them, to whom we owe a considerable debt for their contributions to the transformation of society, come quickly to mind. In the Western sphere, they include Charles Kingsley, F. D. Maurice, J. H. Oldham, William Temple, Abraham Kuyper, Nico Stufkens, Richard and Reinhold Niebuhr, Paul Lehmann, Harvey Cox, Richard Shaull, John C. Bennett, Charles West, J. J. Buskes, Jürgen Moltmann, Johannes Baptist Metz, J. M. de Jong, H. M. Kuitert. In Asia there are Masao Takenaka, M. M. Thomas, Paul Devanandan, T. B. Simatupang, O. Notohamidjojo, and others. In Africa, the name of Adeolu Adegbola must be mentioned. In Latin America there are, among others, Emilio Castro, Rubem Azevedo Alves, Julio Santa Ana, Hiber Conteris, and Maurico Lopez.

It has to be encouraging that men in the so-called developing countries are teaching us a great deal about a theology of transformation. What makes their contribution specially significant is that they work out of a postrevolutionary situation, as in Asia and Africa, on one hand, and out of a prerevolutionary situation, as in Latin America, on the other. The thoughts of these men are molded from experience that reaches far outside their libraries, and for this reason have accents that differ from their Western and Northern colleagues.

While we cannot go into contributions made by all of the writers mentioned, we should underscore the work of two contemporary writers, Johannes Baptist Metz and Jürgen Moltmann.

Johannes Baptist Metz, an ethical theologian who works within the Roman Catholic Church, wrote his *Theology of the World* (1968) to plead for a "political theology." He wants a theology in which the relationship between the church and the world is set within an eschatological framework. The church is in the world, but has its eye on the coming Kingdom and is in fact itself an anticipation of the Kingdom. Thus, if the orthodoxy of belief does not make itself credible through an ortho-*practice* within social and political realities, if the church does not *do* the truth that it proclaims, it is denying its Lord.

Metz sums up his political-theological thoughts in an article that appeared in the journal *Concilium* (4/6) in 1968, on "The Problem of a Political Theology." The kernel of his argument rests on the biblical insight that salvation is never a purely private matter. The public proclamation of salvation drove Jesus into a life-and-death struggle with the political powers. "His cross was not erected in the inner sanctum of individual, personal existence. It did not stand in a holy of holies of a purely religious arena." The cross stands "outside," as Hebrews puts it—outside the threshold of the private life. The Christion church, he contends, in the service of the Kingdom of God carries a critical and liberating form of public responsibility. Hence, a political theology is imperative. Political theology has to define anew for our time the relation between religion and society, church and public life, eschatological faith and social structure. Theology has to do its part in the formation of an eschatological message that is appropriate for the present situation in our society. Since Karl Marx, we have been obligated to lay out the relation between theory and practice, between faith's convictions and social practices, from the perspective of Christian commitment. This is not a politicizing of faith. It is a call to exercise the *critical functions* of faith over against our society.

Jürgen Moltmann's thoughts in a piece called "Toward a Political Hermeneutic of the Gospel" are much like those of Metz. Both theologians bear down hard against the tendency toward individualism in recent Protestant theology. They see form criticism's entanglement with existentialism as a catastrophe. Demythologizing, they contend, ought to be matched by a de-individualizing. Religion becomes a merely private matter whenever God and salvation are turned into the private possibilities of individual existence, and when the eschatological message is narrowed down to a symbolical paraphrase of one's personal doubts and one's private decision-making. Demythologizing demands the price of an unworldly existence coupled with a purely private subjectivity. The result appears in a free-floating sort of preaching that carries within it no trace of the gospel's imperatives for life in society.

Thus the literature of the theology of politics gives evidence of a growing awareness that co-responsibility for society is laid on the Christian community, and that theologians bear a share of the burden, a share that can be accepted by providing biblical insights into the theological grounds for social renewal and, at the same time, suggesting a methodology for how to begin it.

THEOLOGICAL PERSPECTIVES

A. Themes That Need Development

1. Collective, Institutional, and Structural Sin

The common notion of sin is limited far too often to individual transgression of the law and to the intra-psychic life of the sinner. This is unbiblical.

The Bible repeatedly points out that sin is more than rebellion within the heart of man. It tells us that sin works itself out in the collective behavior of groups, classes, nations, and that unrighteousness takes form in institutions and social structures. The prophets of Israel thundered about the structures of Assyria and Babylon, as well as the unrighteousness of Judah and Israel as nations. There are power structures in which unrighteousness takes shape and form, structures in which racism finds its permanent quarters and in which hardness of heart is embodied. Humanists have seen, better than pietistic Christianity, the depths of sin in the structures of feudalism, slavery, colonialism, and imperialism.

Reinhold Niebuhr was one theologian who opened our eyes to this fact. He put the economic imperialism of the United States and the political imperialism of Soviet Russia to the touchstone of the law and the prophets, and in doing so expressed the spirit of the prophets of Israel. It is time again for theology to interpret the collective, institutional, and structural dimensions of human sin. To do this, we must rid ourselves of the stereotyped resistance to concrete identification of institutionalized injustice—racism, for example—that reinforces itself with the notion that sin lies in the human heart and not in social structures. It is possible to pronounce weightily on the authority of God's Word and meanwhile to slip from under its real and living authority whenever that Word speaks to structures as well as to individual men.

2. Divine Judgment on Collective and Structural Sins

The church has tended to specialize in judgment on individual sins. The pulpit has not been heard much proclaiming divine judgment on sinful structures. Strange that this should be so, because the Bible does it all the time. In fact, judgment on collective powers is more typical of the Bible than judgment on individuals. Think of how Assyria, Babylon, Edom, Jerusalem, Samaria, and the like, were constant targets of biblical indictment. The prophets sent a steady stream of prophetic woe over entire nations and societies.

We may also recall the striking and frequently misread story of Jesus' cursing of the barren fig tree (Matthew 21:18-22). How are we to understand it? A tree, in the Bible, is a symbol for certain structures and institutions as is the word "house," e.g., "the house of David." The cursing of the fig tree that bore no fruit is a sign that the structures, whether political, social, economic, or churchly, that do not live up to their responsibility of love and justice, and thus are unfruitful for God, are ripe for judgment. The entire Bible is replete with this sort of situation, from the judgment on Sodom and Gomorrah in Genesis to the judgment on the entire structural complex of Babylon in the book of Revelation (cf. Rev. 18).

This biblical dimension is theologically underdeveloped. And the times now demand that the biblical truth of divine judgment on structural sins gets the attention it deserves from theology. Writers like Niebuhr and, more recently, Richard Shaull have helped us by showing that there are times in history when judgment is ripe for certain obsolete social structures, when the old structures are collapsing and new ones must replace them. We may not agree with the reading of how the new is in fact replacing the old, as, for instance, Shaull offers in his *Encounter with Revolution* (1955); but we must admit that he is asking the right questions about God's judgment in history. Amos and Jeremiah were his predecessors.

3. The Meaning of Reconciliation for Society

The New Testament sees the church as Christ's ministry of reconciliation. "We are ambassadors of Christ, God making his appeal through us. We beseech you on behalf of Christ, be reconciled to God" (II Corinthians 5:20). What is clear from Paul's letters is that this reconciliation "to God" spreads out into the life of men together in society, in their families, their marriages, their racial relations, and their social-economic relations. Reconciliation has a horizontal as well as a vertical dimension. In Ephesians 2, Paul has his eye on Jew-Gentile relations. In I Corinthians 7, reconciliation touches the relation of husband and wife. In Galatians he applies the principle of reconciliation in a situation where race relations were extremely sensitive (Galatians 3–4).

God, who in Christ turned us from the status of enemies to that of friends, and thus healed our broken fellowship, is occupied with a peace offensive that He means to affect our whole lives, in all the nooks and crannies of our world. The first dimension gets the greater stress in the New Testament; peace with God has priority over peace among men, to be sure. And this gives us the greater cause to keep interhuman relationships within the scope of reconciliation.

In its *Book of Confessions* (1967) the United Presbyterian Church has included an article on "Reconciliation in Society" in which the ministry of reconciliation is specifically applied to relations between men and women, rich and poor, as well as between races. It is an exemplary statement, and fittingly set within a churchly confession.

The stress on the ministry of reconciliation as applying to human relations is a sign of the times. In my judgment, the church in its theology, to say nothing of its practice, stands only at the threshold of working out the meaning of reconciliation for the transformation of society.

4. Structural Conversion

The word conversion, so home-grown in the Bible, has been confined by evangelical theology almost wholly to the inner psychic life of individual persons, or to radical change in personal relations with other individuals. But the Bible also uses it in reference to nations and societies: peoples and structures are called to conversion. That the connection, however, between personal and structural conversion is being developed in current theology is reason for rejoicing. Paul Loffler's study of "Conversion and Social Service" in *The Ecumenical Review* of July 1967 was a valuable service for those who search for biblical light in this direction.

5. *God's Actions in History*

Theology has said a great deal about God's mighty acts in history. We may recall Groen van Prinsterer's adage: "It is written. It is historical." We have already remarked that such slogans about God's actions in past history have often been uncritically used to support the status quo, and thus God's acts and historical events are too uncritically joined. But the cliché of modern theology: "God acts in history," contains elements of truth. The statement should not blind us to the fact that sin and demonic powers are also active in history and in processes of development. But it can be taken to indicate that God is at work in the midst of human confusion, amidst the explosive powers of sin and the demonic powers, at work in judgment and in liberation. He leads history through judgment and liberation to the fulfillment of His Kingdom.

As to criteria for discerning the acts of God we can at least say this: wherever love for God and fellow men takes root and grows, there God is at work, and there the fruits of the Kingdom have begun to blossom.

It may be that churches at certain times in history are breeding nests of hate and human alienation, and that in them none of the fruits of love for God and other men can be nourished. We have got to read the signs of the times, and be willing to discern signals of God's judgment and God's liberating action. That God acts in history is certain: whether we recognize what He is doing is often quite uncertain.

6. *The Fulness of Time*

Jesus Christ came in the fulness of time. In Him, the Kingdom came and the time was fulfilled. But since He is the King of the ages, since the times and circumstances are in His hand, there are also other *chronoi* and *kairoi,* other times, that become full, as God's agenda for a given time is being worked out. History, since the coming of Jesus Christ, is an open, dynamic arena for the working out of God's world liberation movement, and thus is ready for the mission and service of the people of God on earth.

We must keep asking ourselves where the struggle for righteousness according to the Kingdom of God must be pressed *now*. We must keep asking where and how in our world it is being manifest that "The time has come for judgment to begin with the household of God. And if it begins with us, what will be the end of those who do not obey the gospel of God?" (I Peter 4:17).

The time of Livingstone, Shaftesbury, and Wilberforce was time for the struggle against slave trade and the entire structure of slavery. The time of Wichern and Marx was the time to search out new structures in the relationship between capital, management, and labor. Now it is the time, and past time, to struggle with the question of relations between races, and between the rich and poor lands, and the question of war and peace. The time is full. What we need to do now is to take a cold shower, to wake up and begin to act. Jürgen Moltmann reminds us forcefully that history does not consist so much of facts as of chances. Chances can be missed. But they can, with God and in His name, also be seized.

7. *The New Earth*

Eschatology, the theological vision of the coming of the new heaven and new earth, the day of judgment and the day of salvation, the time of the end and the time of beginning— eschatology is too frequently still a matter of how the individual will fare in the day of the Lord. But the Bible's eschatological message points to a new order, a new state of affairs, that will sweep all things in heaven and on earth within its wide embrace. The message of the eschaton focuses on far more than the destiny of individual souls; it has to do with the earth, with the city, with the renewal and restoration of the entire cosmos. To set this out in meaningful ways for our time is one of the urgent jobs of theology.

B. Means and Ends: A Confusion in Social Ethics

We have mentioned several elements within theology that need working out if their significance for our revolutionary times is to be appreciated. As far as ethics is concerned, we will need to devote uncommon energies to social, economic, and political morality. Probably the most confused theme in social ethics is the relation between means and ends in the transformation of society.

The relation between means and ends simply cries out for concentrated concern wherever people wrestle with the social, economic, and political structures of life. Declarations about racial, economic, and other social problems will not be enough as long as we fail to include concrete directions on the *means* to attain the *ends* of justice. And for this, we need some tough thinking on the relation that means have to ends. The end does not justify the means. Immoral means cannot achieve moral ends. On the other hand, no worthy ends at all can be achieved unless means are found and exploited.

This question has been on the agenda persistently in the history of Europe. Crisis situations always raise the question among citizens whether it is justified for them, individually or collectively, to overthrow the established government when the practices of the government have become unbearable.

Calvin's disciples, Amesius and Althusis, among others, who were given the label of monarchomachians, objected to the French jurist Bodin for defending the absolute authority of the French monarchs. Bodin affirmed that even tyrants were to be obeyed in all matters. Calvin and his disciples argued that some situations could exist that called for resistance, and that violent revolution could be justified as a last measure in those instances where resistance was called for. Violent revolution, then, was the means that could be used when all other means had failed; it was the *ultima ratio*.

Calvin makes this clear in his *Institutes,* Book IV, Chapter 20. The same thesis can be found in the Calvinistic Helvetian Confession (Art. 30) and the Scottish Confession of 1560 (Art. 14). Calvin's disciples appealed to the example of Shadrach, Meshach, and Abednego in their resistance to Nebuchadnezzar (Daniel 3:16-18) and to Peter's word about the duty to obey God rather than men (Acts 4:19). Biblical passages like these will be looked at later in this book.

The problem of revolution had a very different setting in the sixteenth-century Reformation, or even in Bonhoeffer's resistance against Hitler, than it does in the case of revolutionary movements in developing countries like many in Latin America. The question in these places is not primarily one of whether violent revolution can be accepted as a final measure, but a question of *how* the need for change, transformation, or radical shift in course can be introduced into a society that is hardly conscious of the need or even the possibility of transformation, and of what means are most appropriate for bringing such societies into movement in the direction of renewal. In societies like these the question is how the structures of life can be transformed so that bloody revolutions can be avoided. This is the question on which the concern of Christian people must be focused.

We may be grateful that sober Christian thinking is following these lines. At Uppsala, for instance, when the youth delegates made a declaration on the question of nonviolent vs. violent revolution, they showed no inclination at all to glorify violent revolution or to advocate the ideology of sanculottism. Though violent revolution was not ruled out under all circumstances, the emphasis was totally on means of transformation short of violence.

What follows now is a series of summary remarks on the general question of means in the struggle toward transformation of society.

1. Political, Social, and Economic Development

To provide a society with the dynamic for movement in the direction of renewal, the first requirement is education of the mature members of society. The Latin American Christian philosopher Hiber Conteris, of Uruguay, speaks of how urgent it is for peoples to be made aware of their own situation, in which they otherwise live unconsciously. He argues that the first thing necessary is maturity, the pursuit of understanding and insight into the structures that define their lives, and then conscious commitment to action on the basis of an analysis of their own situation.

One of the elementary needs in most developing countries is the presence of a *model* to show the possibilities of arriving at concrete programs and plans. Such societies have no need of demagogues and adventurers who play with the feelings of the masses. What they do need is sober educators who can conscientiously stimulate the process of consciousness-growth and from there lead the people to think in terms of concrete plans. The people have no need for seducers who exploit the masses for their own ends, nor for autocrats who look down on the masses from their privileged heights. What they do need is men and women who are moved by the situation in which the masses are caught to devote themselves to the education of the people on every level: in educational institutions, in learning centers, in universities, and in forming cadres for political and labor union activities.

2. The Revitalizing of Parliamentary Democracy

On the way to the transformation of the structures of society, the means offered by parliamentary democracy can be exploited in some lands far more effectively than is usually done. Much that has happened in Western Europe can serve as an example. After the revolution of 1848, the framework of parliamentary democracy came into its own. At the time, the liberal elites who created this framework were hardly aware that the people left behind, the exploited and humiliated groups of society, would one day, slowly but surely, learn to use parliamentary democracy in order to transform political democracy into an economic, social, and cultural democracy.

These groups were, in 1848, still hardly aware of the possibilities, and thus were completely unorganized. So the liberal elite, which considered itself the "thinking element of the nation," could hardly imagine the emancipation process that was coming into being, a process that would lead to a whole new ordering of the relationship between capital, management, and labor, to say nothing of the emancipation of the little people, or the liberation of women.

What happened in Europe ought to serve as a model, especially in Latin America. At the beginning of the last century, many countries in Latin America went through a political upheaval that led to formal decolonization and laid the groundwork for political independence and parliamentary democracy. The statues of Simon Bolivar (1783-1830) which one sees everywhere in Latin America witness to this. Bolivar laid the foundation for democracy in several Latin American countries, as he strove to realize the ideals of Jefferson and Montesquieu. It is not to be denied, however, that in most of these countries parliamentary democracy is mere form and façade. They are really ruled by military juntas and tiny oligarchies, who divide power among themselves like Olympic gods while showing no concern at all for the confused masses that fill the cities.

The gap between the old elites and the large masses in urban areas is enormous. The large groups in the cities came in from the country regions and, once within the cities, gradually became the vanguard of the new student generation, leaders of the labor movement and of the newer political parties. In such situations there are better possibilities of using the means available within the structure of parliamentary democracy than is admitted by the men who claim that violence is the only available means of bringing about change. In Bolivia, Colombia, Argentina, Brazil, and Venezuela, to mention only a few of these countries, there are young intellectuals who are now devoting themselves to educational work among the masses, forming cadres, training leaders for labor unions and political parties, working to pave a way to the use of the means of democracy to change the structure of oligarchy.

There are, that is, men who are committed to the transformation of the structures of society, but who are convinced that the first step toward transformation is the creation of a social and political awareness among the people.

Some West Europeans tend to romanticize figures like Che Guevara, offering violent revolution as the only means of change while they denigrate those who are committed to working patiently at developing a social and political awareness among the mass of people, and thus to setting movements loose that may lead to some form of social, political, and economic democracy. The work being done by labor leaders like Maspro of Argentina, by the leaders of the *Movimento Educacio de Base* in northern Brazil, by the *Centro Intercultural de Documentation* in Mexico, by Emilio Castro of Uruguay and by his friends in other parts of Latin America, by some progressive Christian-democrats in Chile and in Venezuela, and by various other neosocialist movements in these countries, deserves far more respect and attention than it now receives. These movements put their heaviest accent on humanization, including their choice of strategic means. Moreover, they are striving toward the energizing and revitalizing of parliamentary democracy. This is an urgent demand all over the world, in the north as well as the south, and deserves respect where it is seriously worked for.

In the midst of the almost sadistic glorification of violence that pervades the world today, it is edifying to listen to the voice of M. M. Thomas of India, present chairman of the Central Committee of the World Council of Churches. To understand Thomas' significance, it must be remembered that he represents one of the "southern" nations, that he has worked for transformation in the social structures from the time of his youth, and that he was speaking in Eastern Europe when he warned against violence.

It was on April 5, 1968, at the Prague Peace Conference, that Thomas protested against the notion being spread about there that the nations of the third world had only three models to choose from: Moscow, Peking, or Havana. He added that in many situations a basic change in the power structure could be effected by revitalizing democracy and the legal procedures built into it. The faddish assumption that democratic methods bring no results and solve no problems and that therefore violent revolution is the only alternative, he said, was nothing other than fatalism. He pointed out that structural means had to be built into the strategies for change in the social and political situations so that chaos could be prevented and the real purposes of renewal could be actually achieved. These purposes include expanding and intensifying the people's participation in the exercise of power and authority, and preventing the formation of new privileged elites as has happened in communistic and neofascist lands. The realization of authentic human goals does not happen by itself, nor just because power is passed from the hands of one group into the hands of another. The goals must be worked for beyond the moment when the revolution or transformation has taken place.

Recent history offers a flood of evidence that whenever a revolutionary process involves destruction of humanity, the goal of the revolution is betrayed. This is why, Thomas argued, concern for what is human must be central in the choice of means in any strategy of change. If we fail to keep central our concern for what is humane, revolution will be betrayed from within and become a new tyranny. Stalinism as well as fascism are writings on the wall of history. We must learn, Thomas said, to develop strategy that will give structural expression to our concern for what is human, to our respect for people within the societies whose wounds we seek to heal.

Thomas' plea for the revitalizing of democracy was gripping. Parliamentary democracy can deteriorate into a soulless ornament. A democracy at any time may become weak and stagnant through lack of communication and situational realism. But this does not call for scrapping democracy. It summons us instead to the task of bringing it back to life.

Within the third world, the seeds exist for a revitalized democratic structure. The seeds are almost destroyed by totalitarian systems (as in China and Latin America), or by oligarchies that refuse to share their own democratic privileges with majority or minority groups within the country (as in South Africa). So it belongs to everyone concerned for the humanity of men to find ways to nourish the seeds of democracy wherever they do exist.

3. Opposition by Word and Action

Several forms of public opposition can be used to hasten the struggle for the renewal of society, all of them trailblazers toward changes in the structure and style of national life.

Exploiting the means offered by the democratic system is not the only possibility. The system is often deaf and dumb, and is moved to respond only after the public conscience is awakened by petition and demonstration. Our time belongs to the mass media, and it is no secret that the media have been the trumpets of demagogues. But anyone who hungers and thirsts after justice has the same media at his disposal, and has an enormous responsibility to exploit them to throw the light of truth on injustice and prod people to enlist in the struggle against it.

The Bible tells us that a day is coming when everything will be set in the light, for all unrighteousness to be judged. The media could be a signal of that light. A journalist friend of mine tells me that he interprets his own vocation as an anticipation of the Day of judgment. Journalism, he believes, has a heavenly calling to open men's eyes, to shake the sleeping into wakefulness, and to sound a reveille for the spiritually dead. Here, it seems to me, is a Christian sense of journalism. What is desperately needed around the world are journalists and commentators who know how to serve the cause of justice and truth through their respective media. What they can accomplish is already evident through isolated instances in Latin America, Asia, and Africa, where many journalists are educating and stimulating masses through courageous reporting and interpreting.

Protest demonstrations are another legitimate means of public opposition. I grew up in a Christian family in which the people's protest for freedom in Dutch education, led by Groen van Prinsterer in 1878, was commemorated every year. I have never lost my admiration for that despised group of little people who arose in the Netherlands against the injustice practiced then against free, Christian education. Theirs was an authentic protest movement, and it succeeded. But now new and different items are on the agenda.

Protest movements in the poor as well as the wealthy countries are aimed at mobilizing public opinion; as such they can be effective in changing the structures. They tend to keep the system off balance, and, like an alarm that may go off at any time, keep society from sleeping too soundly. Radicals within the political parties can hold the urgent issues of war and peace in the world under the noses of the parties until the machine is compelled to deal with them positively.

In this connection, a word should be said about the positive side of youth unrest and the student rebellion. At the World Council meetings in Uppsala I was deeply impressed by the cathartic and renewing significance that the judgments of youth have in all nations. The student rebellions have also had, it must be admitted, a negative and destructive side to them since 1968. Some of the movements were tendentious and faddist more than they were serious efforts to change things for the better. Symptoms of anarchism and syndicalism were present in many student protests. Sometimes violence was toyed with in an utterly irresponsible way. It often seemed as though something magic happened at one's twenty-fifth birthday: before the age of twenty-five a person was by nature a student leader; afterward he magically became a demagogue. Students, it can be said, have acted like the Greeks of Acts 17, who had time to fill the scene with a lot of hot air because their slaves were doing the hard, hand-dirtying daily toil. Negative aspects of the student revolt, wherever it appeared, simply had to be admitted by anyone who viewed it dispassionately.

But there was also something positive about it. It was born of a sense that our world community was splitting at the seams, that it would fall apart unless we really attacked the vital questions of where the world was heading, unless we together said No to racism, to international injustice, to the piling up of atomic weapons, and the like. Young people refused to play the role of uncritical consumers. They really wanted to find out what we of the wealthy West intended to do with our affluence; they wanted to break with the uncritical assumption that the best thing in life was to own and consume things. The youth of the developing lands, too, were no longer of a mind dutifully to accept the structures of injustice that prevailed in places like Latin America. All this must be admitted as a positive force.

That youth of all races and from all cultures often understand each other, without words, in their deepest intentions, has to be one of the most hopeful phenomena in our present world. What has to happen now is for these positive tendencies to move in the direction of a positive renewal of society. That this will happen is not something we can take for granted. The youth protest may just as likely peter out in blind anarchy and lead to devolution instead of revolution.

The direction that the youth protest takes will depend, among other things, on the question of whether the older generation comprehends the deeper motives of the movement and decides to work with the young for genuine renewal. If that happens, perhaps the young will ask themselves why their criticism seems so often to stop at protest against the establishment and so seldom takes the form of constructive proposals that can be evaluated in their own right.

In any case there are in our time profound rumblings that can be heard around the world. The foundations are shaking. Everything is in movement. Whether the movement takes the direction of renewal or destruction is a matter the present generation of young people will have to determine in the future.

4. Nonviolent Resistance

Nonviolent resistance has gradually become a model in the struggle for transformation of society, a model that more and more people are ready to follow. Actually, nonviolent resistance is as old as the prophets of Israel and the apostles of the New Testament. The symbolic acts Jeremiah used to protest against the current political policies of the kings of Judah, the marketplace sermons of Amos in Samaria, the donkey ride into Jerusalem by our Lord, the apostolic warnings against injustice—these were all forms of protest against the existing orders. But the method was one of suffering, of self-denial, of nonviolent resistance.

Barabbas represented anyone who ever took the blood of others to realize his ends. He stood there over against Jesus Christ, who instead gave His own blood for many. Jesus lived amid zealots who expected their dreams to come true only through the sword. He lived amid Herodians who lived by compromise and opportunistic concessions to the unrighteous status quo. Our Lord never encouraged His disciples to accept the way of the zealots. Neither did He suggest they adopt the policies of the Herodians. But He did proclaim the way of the coming Kingdom as the way of cross-bearing and self-denial, of suffering and of passive resistance.

It was this method and this way that gradually set dynamite beneath the violent injustice of the Roman Imperium. In the course of church history many followed the way of non-violence and let their offered lives stand as signals of light through dark centuries. Francis of Assisi and Raymund Lull demonstrated the image of Christ more authentically by their nonviolence during the crusades, when Christian sword encountered Moslem sword, than did the violent methods of Innocent III. The Waldensians, the Albigensians, the Mennonites and Quakers have shown a life-style and demonstrated a method of protest that savors more of the Christian spirit than many another Christian group that has trusted in violence and whose histories are rife with examples of the misuse of power. God has given modern figures, too, who have adopted and demonstrated the power of nonviolence.

It would be inaccurate to list Mahatma Gandhi among the disciples of Christ. He was a Hindu to the end. But Gandhi is undeniably the inspiration for nonviolent resistance in our time. And it is just as undeniable that he borrowed his style of nonviolence from the Sermon on the Mount, from which he frequently quoted to the crowds in India. In South Africa, Christus Luthuli practiced a method of nonviolent resistance until he died, and he has many who today follow his example in that sad land. The same is true in South-West Africa, the country that today is unjustly subject to the jurisdiction of South Africa. One of the resistance leaders there is Toivo Herman Ja Toivo. Toivo declared in a Pretoria court in 1968 that he was opposed to violence; but he added that he had, in desperation, given support to some who saw violence as the only voice that would be heard in a situation in which "we were voiceless in our own land and robbed of any means to give form to our political convictions." Today, though, more men are taking Luthuli's route.

Nonviolent resistance can hardly be mentioned today without giving attention to Martin Luther King. King's dream was the dream of Israel's prophets. His heart and mind were full of the prophets' message to Israel. Anyone reading King's speeches must be struck with the way passages like Isaiah 11 and 65, along with so many others, were deeply a part of him. His dream was really that of the new earth wherein righteousness dwells. But the dream was not a romantic vision for King; it was biblical hope.

The cross and resurrection of Jesus were the bridgehead for a world in which racial, economic, cultural, and political justice would finally prevail. King's perspective was aimed nearby, at real people, but it was at the same time thrown out beyond, way beyond the present to the new world that came and is still to come with Jesus Christ.

But King was also a man with a method. His method was nonviolent resistance. King grasped how important it was to keep means consistent with ends. In this he had learned from Gandhi. I recall an observation made by Shahrir, the Indonesian nationalist who did so much to stop the bloodletting during Indonesia's struggle for independence, after he had talked with Gandhi: "This man was so sure, so pure, and so joyful because he knew that his end was pure and that his methods were morally right." King was the same way. Holding the line against critics from all sides, the side of violence and the side of reaction, he persisted in his nonviolent resistance because he would rather fail with the right method than use methods that would corrupt his ends.

Viewed by a European, King's method may be summed up in the following way:

(1) *Direct action to dramatize an unjust situation.* The situation was first well analyzed. King never used hysterical, inflated images; he never stooped to slander. The procedure was always the same: careful researching of the situation, then a dramatic demonstration to awaken public conscience.

(2) *Direct action after talk breaks down.* He followed this rule he set for himself: "One goes into direct action after talk has gone on as long as possible. We seek to win our opponents to our cause. We do not seek to defeat them. If nothing is won at the conference table, we must first purify ourselves. We must begin to act only as we surely know that we love our enemies for Christ's sake." King's method reveals an understanding of men illumined by the cross of Christ. He did not live by extremes; to him the devils were not all on one side and the angels all on the other. He knew the pride of the "haves" and he knew the rage of the oppressed; he knew the humanity they had in common, a humanity that could be recognized by both sides only as both passed through the valley of forgiveness, reconciliation, and renewal.

(3) *Acceptance of suffering.* Love, he said, will bring us to places where we will be denied. This will cause suffering. "We know," he said, "that to win a revolution we must often walk through streams of blood. We will see to it that the blood of others will never be shed by us." He sometimes recalled I Peter 2:19-24: "For it is a fine thing if a man endure the pain of undeserved suffering because God is in his thoughts. What credit is there in fortitude when you have done wrong and are beaten for it? But when you have behaved well and suffer for it, your fortitude is a fine thing in the sight of God. To that you were called, because Christ suffered on your behalf, and thereby left you an example." This is the love that conquers the world. And it must be said that the power of nonviolent resistance, reflecting suffering love, is stronger than the violence of the powerful.

(4) *Reconciliation as the purpose of action.* The end of our action, King insisted, was reached only when the conflict-

ing parties were wholly reconciled to each other. There could be no victors. There could only be reconciled men. As the example of King dims, and other more violent voices prevail, one thing remains certain: when we one day ask which method touched human conscience most deeply and which method gave strongest impulse toward conversion and renewal, we will not have long to wonder.

In the long run, the method of nonviolent resistance has the longest staying power and the deepest influence because in it the relationship between means and ends reflects the way God takes toward His own future Kingdom.

In Latin America, Dom Helder Camara, the Archbishop of Recife, has also opted for the method of nonviolent resistance, and in so doing follows in the steps of Gandhi and King. Camara has chosen this method because he is convinced Jesus Christ directs him to do it. But he is also pragmatic, and senses that a strategy of change is more effective in the long haul than a strategy of violent upheaval. Camara's nonviolent movement, Justice and Peace, was endorsed by the Brazilian national conference of bishops in 1969, and has chapters all over Brazil as well as other countries. The movement in Brazil takes the form of a pressure group against what Camara calls internal and external colonialism in Brazil's economy, colonialism carried on both by feudal powers within the country and by North American exploitation from without. But the pressure is directed also against the arrest of innocent people and the torturing of prisoners—a quality that is still present in Brazil.

Camara still has no entrance into the heavily censured press or other mass media, and all of his educational material has to be distributed clandestinely. But outside of Brazil he uses his growing influence to plead openly for changes in the economic structures of life as well as in the political and ecclesiastical systems.

My point is not to repeat Camara's ideas here, but only to indicate his method, his technique for bringing about social and political renewal. It is passive resistance, the method of social education, of setting in movement new influences to effect concrete reformations on a small scale and thus prepare the people for larger and more significant change. There is a slogan afoot among some revolutionaries to the effect that we should create two or three more Vietnams; Camara rejects such slogans as viciously counterproductive. But he does not take up the argument against revolutionary violence from the side of a lethargic pietism; he does not condemn violence with his own arms folded. While he denounces violence, he points to what he believes is the better way to realize the dream of justice—a dream he shares with King and millions of others.

In this same connection, we may recall Prague in August of 1968. Czechs young and old that month were meeting Russian tanks with passive, nonviolent resistance. The Czechs did not set tanks against tanks, but met the invasion courageously with passive defense. Secret radio, political cartoons, imprisonment, demonstrations, strikes, boycotts, unarmed encounters with the Russians, and occasional martyrdom—all these seemed more powerful to the Czechs at the time than anything in their arsenal. There are indications that what happened there got home to the Russians, all the way to the heart of Moscow. This kind of resistance did make a profound impression in Russia, and continues to ferment there as a hope for greater liberty, even though we know that the Czech passive resistance was put down in blood, and that those who hoped for liberation from the almighty state have gone down into a tunnel of even tougher oppression.

For some, the lesson of Prague is that passive civil resistance has no glimmer of chance. I think it is the other way around. The Prague leaders had no time for preparation. They had to improvise on the spot, and did what they could in a situation that was hopelessly determined from the beginning. As Adam Roberts remarked, the collapse of this resistance lay in its lack of preparation, the failure of leadership, and the vacuum of theoretical forethought. The lesson of Prague must be that preparation, leadership, and theoretical (as well as practical) analysis must precede a resistance movement. In the future, ministers of defense will have to create an apparatus for passive resistance in situations where a country is overrun by brute force. Centers will have to be established where resistance to unjust governments and power structures can be thought through carefully.

The methods of passive resistance have been enormously reinforced by what has happened in the civil rights struggle in the United States and by what happened in Prague. These have become models that can be used to stimulate change on a far wider and deeper scale in the future.

It must be said that no method should be absolutized. We must not suppose that no situation could ever come about that might call for the use of limited violence. Gandhi did not absolutize nonviolence. He recognized his technique as a moral means of reaching moral ends, but he also saw it as a specific strategy that, in the Indian situation, had the best long-term chance of success. He was aware that other situations could arise that called for other strategies. The same was true of King. He was sometimes criticized for turning his vision into a dogma that was too simplistic for the complicated reality of the black struggle. But King's answer was that, in a land where civil rights were juridically grounded, and in which the highest courts determined rights, the method of passive resistance was the most effective way to bridge the gap between official rights and the actual state of affairs where rights were frustrated in practice. Until his death, King worked at this method; but he never denied that situations might exist in which other methods would be needed.

The leaders of Prague in 1968, too, were aware that over against the real threat of horrible bloodletting and massive deportation, irenic passive resistance was the only way to translate into action what had begun to live in the hearts of Czech people. That is, their passive resistance was chosen for that situation. But there are other situations, and they raise the question of whether other methods do not have more chance of success, and whether it is morally permissible to refuse to use other methods than passive resistance.

5. General Strikes

One means that should not be too quickly dismissed in certain situations is that of the general strike. A general strike can be a profound protest against any unbearable denial of a people's humanity; it can be a cry for justice. In the Netherlands we still remember the general strike of 1941 with pride; it was at that time a piercing cry against the slaughter of Jewish people. As we recall it, we now realize that it was the smallest possible expression of our sharing in the lot of the Jews. Afterward our only regret was that it could not have been more effective, more powerful, more extensive; if we had only gotten the police and all of the railroad people to go along with it, we might have accomplished more. When inhumanity reaches a climax and the situation becomes humanly intolerable, a general strike by the armed forces, the police, and the utility people can be a means to change without bloodshed. It is effective because it is a means to cripple the power apparatus and pave the way for seizure of power.

6. Violent Revolution as a Last Resort

In everything we have said thus far, we have agreed with those who have stressed the Christian responsibility to dig in for justice and, to that end, to work for changes in structures in which injustice is invested, to seek creatively for and to apply nonviolent methods of change. Nonviolence obviously is of a piece with the Spirit of Jesus Christ. Besides, history clearly teaches us that violence more often than not only leads to new forms of despotism and tyranny.

But we cannot stop here. The present world situation is so urgent that the question must be faced as to whether, in some situations, a limited measure of violence does not belong to the list of possible methods of change. The urgency of the question is reflected in ecumenical discussions.

At the Conference on Church and Society in Geneva, violence as a final measure was mentioned only in passing. Nonviolent methods were again endorsed at the Conference of Zagorsk in 1968, but the possibility of minimum violence was also suggested; "we must realize," the conference report said, "that there are situations in which Christian groups must act in full awareness of their responsibility to participate in a revolution along with the violence that may accompany it." The papal encyclical *Progressio populorum,* of 1967, warns that violent revolution usually does more harm than good; but it does not rule out the necessity of violence absolutely. Uppsala (1968) underscored the endorsement of nonviolence, but also admitted that in intolerable situations conscience may compel Christians to participate in violent revolution. At Notting Hill (1969) and at the conference that took place in Baden-Baden (1970), it was observed that impatience was growing intense among many peoples and that Christian ecumenical circles were being urged not to make nonviolence a new dogma.

The background of this subtle shift of accent is easy to see. The spiral of violence and counterviolence has intensified in recent years. A tidal wave of reactionary powers is beating the beaches of current history. An aggressive colonialism is stiffening in several places: Mozambique, Angola, Guinea. With assistance from the United States, reactionary military coups have been organized with the purpose of holding on to the status quo. Great powers are maintaining their hege-mony over regions with brute force—as Russia did in Czecho-slovakia and as China did in Tibet. Racist regimes, like South Africa and Rhodesia, perpetuate their power monopolies with structured violence.

Many Christians are counted among those who refuse to accept their lot any longer and who have become convinced that violence must be part of their strategy. If we listen to their explanations for their decisions, we will hear things like this: Those who make a dogma of nonviolence forget that al-most every significant change in social structures has come about through violent revolution: the Netherlands (80-year war), the United States, France, Russia, England, all of them have come through revolution. Why, they ask, must we be forbidden to use the means that played so crucial a role in your own history?

Those who opt for violence also respond to their judges by accusing them of naiveté, for not seeing that the question of *who* the shapers of political change are going to be cannot be evaded. Finally, we hear the complaint that those who plead for gradual and nonviolent improvement are themselves frequently the reason why revolutionaries get impatient and begin to expect salvation from violent assault.

Complaints like these are heard more frequently these days —from the ghettoes of American cities, from freedom movements in South Africa, from guerillas in Latin America. Anyone who has known living relationships with people who faced the decision of violence in the anticolonial wars is not able to ignore the complaints one hears now.

The World Council of Churches and the Vatican can function as catalysts in serious consideration of the question of violence. They demonstrate (through Sodepax—the united committee for "Society, Development, and Peace") that they are not of a mind to ignore the questions and criticisms raised by the impatient proponents of violent revolution. In this way, they are saying that the churches and theology now have a greater responsibility than ever to consider the question of strategy for the renewal of societies, and to put urgent questions before those whose lot it is to lead others into action.

For this, the first need is situational realism. The question of strategy for change can be profoundly asked only after the situation has been realistically studied. Secondly, the church and theology must raise the question of whether all other means have really been exhausted. Thirdly, they must ask whether the situation is in fact such that violent overthrow of the existing power structures has become an act of obedience to God and of love toward men.

What sort of situation might this be? It may exist where fundamental human rights are no longer built into and protected by the existing structures, but rather are intentionally betrayed and denied by them. Or, it may exist where the government constitutionally affirms human rights, but in practice rejects the constitution by which it is bound. Whenever the government cuts itself off from the constitution under which it exists, it has lost touch with the basis for the state itself. This does not mean that violent revolution is called for whenever this happens. It may be the responsibility of citizens in that time to endure the situation with patience. But situations may also arise—as Calvin saw—in which people are summoned to take the reins of power, and when refusal to seize power is a failure of duty.

What is needed today is a "principle of justified revolution." The traditional principle of the just war has been made obsolete by modern technology. A new principle, this time of the just revolution, must be devised to replace it. In such a statement, the following questions must be answered:

(1) Who are the persons called to take over the powers of government in times when a takeover is necessary?

Karl Barth has said that the church in some situations could be responsible for giving the word for power seizure. There have, in fact, been occasions in which the church did perform this function. In the rebellion against Spain, as well as in other revolutionary situations, the Reformation church had the courage to appoint political deacons who then acted as counsellors to the magistrates. In a country like Brazil, the counsel of bishops could be most useful. Still, the function of the church could never be more than advisory. The church has neither the calling nor the competence to give actual political direction.

Calvin, speaking out of the structures of his contemporary society, argued that lower magistrates had the calling to assume the task of higher magistrates. But this model can hardly serve us in our time. The most important aspect of Calvin's teaching is that politics itself is a vocation, a divine calling, and that those people who know they are called to it by God and the people, and who are qualified to do so, must in some instances take over the function of governing. Taking over the powers of government is a job for neither adventurers nor the unqualified. It is a *calling* for people who are qualified by experience and ability, but more, for people who out of the depths of their conscience can, in Calvin's language, say: "I appeal to God who has called me to this task."

(2) The way of revolution may be taken only if a real possibility exists for exchanging the present "disorderly order" for a more just order. Where that possibility is not present,

revolution is an irresponsible, and actually a reckless, mad adventure doomed to bring misery to countless innocent people. Modern history furnishes ample illustrations to support this statement.

(3) The support of the people must be assured in any legitimate revolution. No revolutionary government can stand without the *consensus populi*. Fidel Castro understood this in Cuba. Che Guevara forgot it in Bolivia, as his diary makes clear.

A revolution begun by a small group of elite or a handful of adventurers is illegitimate. Reinhold Niebuhr saw this plainly when he wrote: "The real question is, what are the political possibilities of establishing justice through violence?" If circumstances have become intolerable and resistance needs to be channeled, the decisive question is whether adequate possibilities are present for gaining justice by means of organized efforts to take over the power of government.

In prerevolutionary periods, when signs point toward upheaval, Christians must ask pertinent questions of revolutionaries. What is your goal? What are the concrete possibilities of achieving your goal? What guarantees have you that your way will not open the door to a new tyranny—or chaos? Questions like these must be asked. Experience and history show us that most revolutions have brought no real improvement in the people's lot, and were actually senseless explosions of violence. But history also provides examples where seizure of power was a powerful form of love.

The stigmata of Jesus of Nazareth are more clearly visible in the ways and means of nonviolent resistance than in the way of violent revolution, even when accepted only as a last resort. But we are given no right to judge those leaders who have grasped the last resort in concrete situations, and we have much reason to think gratefully of those who followed them through all the temptations to which they were vulnerable.

Finally, this note: In the question of revolution, as in all others, we must get back to the center, the summary of the divine law—love to God and love to neighbor. Any revolution is illegitimate, immoral, and irresponsible that is not driven by authentic love for God and people. A revolution is alone law-ful whose leaders are profoundly persuaded, after an ago-nized analysis of the situation, and all other means have failed, that they are compelled by love of God and neighbor to take the road of revolutionary power. For the only way to justice is the way of love. All other roads lead to anarchy, to tyranny, to totalitarian oppression, and never to a new, more just order of life.

7. *The Christians' Task During Revolution*

The role the Christian plays is hardest of all during a revo-lution. Many Christians have had to find their way through this period with fear and trembling. Some are in it now. Their tough task is to warn against sadism on one hand and revolu-tionary romanticism on the other. Their job—as someone else has said—is to de-ideologize the revolution. It is theirs to pre-vent the revolution from turning into a "devouring Moloch." They must keep large and clear before the revolutionary lead-ers that their ultimate task is to organize for peace and recon-ciliation in justice.

To sound these notes during .the upheaval is a formidable task. It is one reason why Christians are often distrusted by both right and left extremists. But if the Christian community suspends its ethical message during the time of upheaval it must not be surprised if it never gets a hearing when the revolution is over. If the Christian ethos is not active while the powers are changing, the new machine is likely to be put into the service not of justice, but of violence, not of renewal, but of destruction.

The followers of Barabbas tend to crowd out the followers of Christ during revolutionary upheaval. But there are many examples, too, in South Africa and Latin America, Indonesia, India, and Pakistan of ordinary and important people, of generals and professional men and women, who have fulfilled a ministry of reconciliation, and have demonstrated that theirs is a passion for justice, for mercy, and for humaneness.

8. *The Christian in the Postrevolutionary Situation*

During a revolution, people are often so caught up in the

question of which means to use to change the situation that they fail to make concrete the ends they want to achieve. The day of revolution is so pressing that they think little of the years that must come afterward.

One of my objections to the kind of theology of revolution espoused by Richard Shaull is that he leaves this question begging in the assumption that the ends of the revolution will clarify themselves in the process of change. This strikes me as a kind of gnosticism. Gnosticism believed that the light would inevitably win the victory over darkness by itself, in its own way, as it emerged through the ongoing struggle. But this is heresy. And it is exposed by experience. Almost every country that underwent revolutionary upheaval after World War II experienced profound frustration; after the surge of revolutionary expectations disillusionment subverted the early élan because no one had planned concretely for rebuilding the machinery of society during the postrevolutionary period. It is this task to which Christians must give themselves with vigor —both to plan and to rebuild after the revolution has occurred.

Every postrevolutionary government is exposed to the temptation to misuse its power as flagrantly as the government it supplanted. It may be that "the mighty shall be cast from their thrones," but the revolutionary easily forgets that he may be tomorrow's "mighty." The new power should be aware that the same temptations to which the *ancien régime* fell victim are going to powerfully assault him as well. Every postrevolutionary leader is tempted to solve the problem of dissent by liquidating his opponents of yesterday. Here is where the Christian must play a role of utmost importance. He must point out to the revolutionary that even though it will take time and enormous effort, reconciliation with former opponents of revolution must be high on the postrevolutionary agenda. The Christian must be alert to the temptation for revolutionists to perpetuate indefinitely the temporary dictatorship intended only to bring order in the interim. In short, the Christian's function is to press for the very fundamental rights and democratic liberties the revolution was all about from the beginning.

Conclusion:

We must learn to live, act, and labor under the dawning light of the Kingdom of God that has come and is coming still. Here, in conclusion, we will let ourselves be grasped again by the biblical vocabulary that summarizes so powerfully the life's posture to which we are called. Two words appear in connection with our expectations of the new earth: *wait* and *hasten*. These are the watchwords that all who await His coming are summoned to obey.

The new earth will be a place where justice between races shall prevail. For this reason we are called to hasten in the struggle against all forms of racial discrimination now, and against all structures in which racial discrimination is institutionalized. And for the same reason, we are called to live along with, work along with, struggle along with those who hunger and thirst after more racial justice.

Our summons to "wait" protects us from bitterness, hate, and fanaticism. Our summons to "hasten" prevents us from resigning ourselves to the status quo.

The new earth is going to be a place in which economic justice shall prevail. This is why we are called to help with the struggle toward a world economy in which the production, distribution, and consumption of goods can bridge the gulf between the rich and poor of the world. This is why we must choose sides for a politics that really does aim at economic justice and at the removal of barricades that stand in the way of realizing it. But in hastening toward economic justice we will not become disillusioned and cynical in reaction to inevitable disappointments in the struggle.

The new earth is going to be a place in which social justice dwells. This is why we must struggle against those structures in which capitalist domination sanctions injustice, or in which dictatorship of management blinds the eyes to social suffering, or in which dictatorship of labor stagnates progress. This is why we must struggle for the kind of social order in which all sharers in the labor of society have a responsible place in a genuine community and in which social concern embraces everyone, to the smallest and weakest members. But in hastening toward social justice we will remember Him who in the last chapter shall wipe the last traces of social injustice from the face of the earth.

The new earth is going to be a place in which cultural justice prevails. This is why we do not intend to make an idol of the status quo in which one group bathes in mild cultural sunshine while the other is imprisoned in cultural darkness. We shall be associated with those who strive to spread cultural wealth over the length and breadth of the earth, bringing to all who inhabit this planet a portion of those cultural goods in which love for God and neighbor can be enriched. But we do not intend to let our hastening cause us to forget to wait on Him who tests all culture with His righteous norms, and who alone builds the New Jerusalem in which culture and worship blend as one forever.

The new earth is going to be a place of political justice and everlasting peace. This is why we struggle against injustice in government and in relations between nations, why we struggle for international order, and for a security system that covers this whole planet. But we shall not forget that we shall have to wait, nor are we going to become cynical in the frustrations of the struggle.

I will not expand on the implications of these sentences. My only point is to hint at what "hastening" and "waiting" can mean in practice if we just stretch our concerns far enough. The Marxist philosopher Ernst Bloch has, in his book *Das Prinzip Hoffnung* (2 vols., 1953, 1956), shown what hope as a principle has meant in human history. But it was never said of Jesus Christ that He is a *principle* of hope. Rather He Himself, the Person, in what He has done, what He does, and what He shall do, is our hope.

There have been periods of history in which Christians experienced at the depths of life what it means for Christ to be their hope. During such times, extraordinary power radiated from His disciples to the world. In other times, Christendom has betrayed Christ our hope by settling for the status quo.

Jürgen Moltmann once observed that pietist Christians tend to decry the evil of the world and then leave the world alone.

But the world is looking for a Christianity that calls the world evil and steps into the world, looks all its evil forms full in the face, and does something to change it.

Proclaiming the coming of the Kingdom is not enough. We are called to wait and to hasten toward the Kingdom of God in the awareness that neither waiting nor hastening is in vain— for we expect a new heaven and a new earth where justice will finally be at home.

PART 2

REVOLUTION
The Fact of History

by
H. G. SCHULTE NORDHOLT*

*What follows grew from a seminar on revolution at the Free University of Amsterdam, led by Dr. Nordholt, professor of cultural anthropology. Students whose contributions to the Seminar were used in preparing these chapters are: A. Rietveld, P. H. Streefland, A. deVries-Van der Linden, and M. Djajadiningrat-Nieuwenhuis.

INTRODUCTION

Revolution is a burning question. Anyone picking it up has to handle it gingerly. This goes for the church, and for social analysts as well. It is perhaps no accident that in the four volumes prepared for the Geneva Conference on Church and Society (1966) the phenomenon of revolution did not appear on the agenda, even though the title of the third volume was *Responsible Government in a Revolutionary Age*. The social sciences, however, are just as skittish. Revolution is not present in the 3000 columns of the huge work called *Theories of Society* (1965), compiled by four of America's leading sociologists, Talcott Parsons, Edward Shils, Kaspar Naegele, and Jesse Pitts.

Revolution is still a fairly new concept. Earlier, it belonged to astronomy. Copernicus, for instance, called his observations *De Revolutionibus Orbium Coelestium*—"On the Revolution of the Heavenly Bodies"—to stress the regularity and ordainedness of the stars. In this sense the word revolution was first borrowed by historians. In England "revolution" was used of the return of the Stuarts to the throne in 1660 (Cromwell's rebellion was *not* a revolution, but the restoration of the monarchy *was* a revolution). The restoration of the old order under William of Orange and Mary Stuart was called the "Glorious Revolution."

Probably the fall of the Bastille on July 14, 1789, set the stage for the modern understanding of revolution. When it happened, Louis XVI said to his minister: "It is a revolt." "No, Sire," came the answer, "it is a revolution." Even then the word meant: like the stars, it is irreversible. But the new notion was breaking through.

A whole complex of ideas broke loose with the French Revolution, central to which was that the world can change radically and that men can break with the past and create a new order. Many cultures have tasted the longing for total change, especially when life has gotten bogged down in the morass of injustice and despair. It is the sighing for a lost paradise, the longing for a golden age. Peoples who have come to know the Judeo-Christian messianic vision have experienced this longing in the promise of the millennium. But they are not alone.

The vision of brighter times plays through all modern revolutionary movements, but with this difference: today's revolutionists do not look back to a golden age; they do not think of rebirth or renaissance, nor of a return to the sources. They are of a different spirit than the Reformers, who wanted a return to the purity of the early church. They are also of another stripe than radical Christians who reject this evil world in the name of the future millennium, God's Kingdom on earth. Modern revolutionists want to create *their* kingdom of the future now.

Concordet confessed his faith in the perfect man of the future in his famed *Historical Table of the Progress of the Human Spirit* of 1793. Comte used his positivistic sociology to develop the notion of human progress even further. But it was Darwin who tied faith in human development to natural evolution. Now the notion of *irresistibility* came back into the notion of revolution—with a vengeance. Revolution was seen not only as an irreversible historical movement, but as a natural movement as irreversible as the stars. With this, the word "revolution" was back with Copernicus.

And here is the inner contradiction of many modern revolutionists: they determined freely to create a new world, but they knew that the way the revolution was to work out was determined beforehand. They knew that the French Revolution was very violent and so they willed violence. They knew that revolutions tend to devour their own children, and yet they fought for freedom. As Hannah Arendt has said, they were "the fools of history."

The New York Times reported that between 1946 and 1959 there were more than 1200 clear instances of civil war, guerilla wars, localized outbreaks of fighting, organized and apparently unorganized terrorism, rebellion, and coups. Only a handful of societies managed to keep their equilibrium in this period of general unrest. But even these, since 1914, have experienced war and more general disturbances.

Is there a pattern to all this that will help us understand the revolution phenomenon? Are there things that we can tie together that reveal that revolution takes place according to some rationally understandable course? In recent years, students have begun to recognize that social conflict, social change, and even social progress do show a correlation among themselves. But social change takes place in a given, specific time. It is a historical process. And social sciences are not necessarily equipped theoretically to do historical research. Social scientists generally have gotten off the Comtian kick of pseudo-historical theories, and have mended the fences of empirical reality as they have it before them. Their tools are "social surveys," experiments in more or less controlled situations by means of empirical methods.

Social *change,* however, is harder to get hold of. Revolutions make things very tough for social scientists with their interview techniques and their charts. Social scientists confronted with radical change in history are thrown off balance. They are like shoemakers who are given a cow and ordered to make leather soles.

History, of course, has always been plagued with conflict, wars, and revolutions. History does not know what to do with peace. Nor do historians.

The solution is to establish a new cooperation between historians and other social scientists, so that they can learn from each other's methods to probe into the general phenomenon of revolution. We are living through a revolutionary period. The people of the developing countries are fascinated by Marxism as they wrestle with the problems precipitated by the processes of modernization. Economic development is often slowest of all to improve. If the economic structure can be revolutionized, according to Marxism, the superstructure of the rest of society —which rests on the economic—will be revolutionized inevitably. This explains the interest of developing countries in economic questions. There is a revolutionary élan very manifest in these places. The ends are not always clear, but the methods often include the method of violence.

This is one reason why churches everywhere, not only in conferences in Geneva, do well to think about the phenomenon of revolution.

1

A DEFINITION OF REVOLUTION

Strangely, it is hard to say what a revolution is. The French Revolution endowed the word with the concrete and clear meaning of a violent and sudden change of political and social structures. Philosophy of law and political science usually define it juridically; for instance, "the seizure of state authority —usually by force—by a person or group with the purpose of bringing about drastic changes in a specific political structure." The possibility of a coup d'etat without the open use of violence is here left open. Chalmers Johnson, in his book *Revolution and the Social System* (1964), takes over Siegmund Neumann's definition: revolution is "a drastic, fundamental change in the political organization, the social structure; it is control of the economic domain, and the dominant myth of the social order, which therewith signals a radical break in the continuity of historical development." But generally, the notion of revolution tends to take in more and more territory, as seen in such phrases as "the industrial revolution." Social sciences see revolution as "a sudden and far-reaching major break in the continuity of development" (*Dictionary of Social Sciences*, 1933). In this broad, general sense, Wendland, at the Geneva Conference on Church and Society, spoke of revolution as nothing more than "modernization."

The large question of what revolution is in any precise sense, then, is left dangling. Social sciences are unable to produce even a fairly precise definition that can be used by everyone. Whenever a given science does define it for itself, its definition only creates confusion when thrown out in the common intellectual marketplace. Hence, many tend to look for new terms instead of for acceptable definitions of old ones. Some have tried the phrase "internal war," as is suggested by Eckstein (H. Eckstein, ed., *Internal War*, 1964). But in this the purpose of radical *social* change is not present. Probably we will be better off if we stick fairly close to a definition of revolution something like that given by the sociologists: "a sudden and far-reaching major break in the continuity of development." It is certainly necessary, as we use the word "revolution" in general, to make clear whether we mean a revolution with violence or one without violence. This is crucial, for practical purposes; for many call themselves revolutionary who would not be thought so by others, and the key difference lies in whether violence is accepted as an ingredient in revolutionary strategy.

2

THE MARKS OF REVOLUTION

We can get closer to understanding revolution by noting some crucial marks of actual revolutions than by making a definition that accounts for all the dimensions, not all of which appear in every revolution. By observing certain basic characteristics we may find it possible to arrive at a kind of revolutionary model. Then, the presence or absence of other marks can help us arrive at a typology of revolution.

A. The Influence of the French Revolution

(1) The most fundamental trait of a revolution is the will to *renewal* and faith in its possibility. All revolutionaries are possessed by a belief that a new epoch is about to break through. Only where this passion for the radically new is present can we truly speak of revolution. The vision of renewal is total; it takes in all the political, social, and economic structures—seen as a whole. A myth must thus be alive, a myth of a total new order, of a new world that can come only by means of an abrupt break with the existing order. The myth must be present to sustain the passion.

(2) Along with the passion for newness, every revolution is heady with *freedom* (freedom and liberation must be kept clearly separated here). The consciousness that an unbearable

yoke must be lifted burdens every revolution. Hence, the road to freedom must pass through liberation. People must be liberated from tyranny, from foreign domination, from an inferior social status, or from economic exploitation, if they are to arrive at freedom. Freedom in its first phase is negative—freedom from something, liberation. Afterward comes the summons to grasp hold of freedom itself. And this is the tragedy of almost all revolutions: liberation is gained, but freedom gets no shape or form.

Hannah Arendt, in her book *On Revolution* (1963), sets the American Revolution in contrast to the French, and concludes that the American Revolution was successful in giving form to freedom because it was a *political* revolution rather than a social revolution. It was not as though no social question existed in the colonies. Some 400,000 people lived in slavery, and the 1,850,000 whites lived in relative prosperity only because of the presence of slave labor. But no one gave a thought to the presence of slaves as a social question. Hence, the colonists were not diverted by social issues from facing the political question. After liberation, freedom was given constitutional form, set in a guarantee of inalienable civil rights and the opportunity to share in the decision-making processes of the state.

France, in contrast, was led to turn away from the ideal of political freedom in order to solve the social question. Robespierre brought new twists into full view when he said: "I know only the social question." The political search for the Rights of Man became a social demand for the rights of the Sans-Culottes. And this change became the model for all revolutions to follow.

The dominating influence the French Revolution has had is a result also of the influence of Karl Marx. The young Marx was convinced that the French Revolution failed to establish freedom because it failed to solve the social question, and this persuaded him that freedom and poverty were irreconcilable. Moreover, poverty, Marx believed, was the result of exploitation by the ruling class. Exploitation was possible because the ruling class had gained control by force of the means of production. Thus, Marx was able to turn the social question into a political instrument, with the word "exploitation" as the rallying cry.

Revolutionary theory, formed on the basis of the French experience, thus made it possible for the French Revolution to serve as the model for all others, in particular the Bolshevik Revolution of 1917.

(3) The idea that the course of revolution is *irresistible* is also a product of the French Revolution. The first phase brings liberation. Thereafter comes the dictator. The revolution must devour its own children in a series of consecutive revolutionary aftershocks. The "suspected" must be exposed. Then come two factions—the "tolerant" and the "enraged"—who work together to subvert the revolutionary leadership. At this stage, the revolution is rescued by a man from among the moderates who in fact turns out to be far from moderate. He liquidates extremists of both left and right, as Robespierre liquidated both Danton and Hebert. The irresistible movement led Hannah Arendt to say: "The magic spell which historical necessity has cast over the minds of men since the beginning of the nineteenth century gained in potency by the October Revolution, which for our century has had the same profound meaningfulness of just crystallizing the best of men's hopes and then realizing the full measure of their despair that the French Revolution had for its contemporaries."

The theory of irresistibility of the revolutionary tidal wave still possesses the spirit of revolutionaries. Fidel Castro is an example. It tends to become more than a theory of how revolutions developed in the past. It becomes a conviction of how revolutions will develop, and thus a self-fulfilling prediction.

(4) Belief in *human goodness* and the stimulus of *pity* were two more marks of the French Revolution.

Christianity confesses that man is sinful. The French Revolution, in tune with philosophers Locke and Rousseau, was backed by the conviction that human nature is good. Moreover, human goodness finds its noblest expression in pity (distinguished from compassion) for the everlastingly miserable people. Pity for the *people*—the people in unlimited generality

—is the peak of human virtue. Always, it is for *the people*, not necessarily for a specific person. But pity, urged as the source of all virtue, turned out to be a larger potential for cruelty than cruelty itself. In the name of pity for humanity it became possible to defend inhumanity to persons.

Hannah Arendt, in this connection, draws on Herman Melville's greatest novel, *Billy Budd*. The problem is that the end of the eighteenth century set Christianity into a crisis such as it had never known before. One crucial stage of the crisis was that the French Revolution was setting about to rectify the original sins of the old world. It turned out to be a bloody reformation, and so the revolution itself was caught in the sinful stream.

Billy Budd is the man of nature, gifted beautifully with "barbaric" innocence. The story is about the goodness that is beyond virtue and the evil that is beyond vice. Goodness, rising from nature's womb, works with power and even with violence. Billy Budd has such goodness, and only his violent killing of a man who had lied about him is adequate for it. *This* goodness relieves man of corruption.

This is how the story begins. Virtue—*not* goodness—is exemplified by Captain Vere. Virtue—in the Captain—stands between absolute goodness and absolute evil. An angel slew the false witness, but the angel had to be hanged for it.

Arendt writes of this: "Clearly, Melville reversed the primordial legendary crime, Cain slew Abel, which has played such an enormous role in our tradition of political thought. But this reversal was not arbitrary; it followed from the reversal the men of the French Revolution had made of the proposition of original sin, which they had replaced by the proposition of original goodness. . . . Let us suppose that from now on the foundation stone of our political life will be that Abel slew Cain. Don't you see that from this deed of violence the same chain of wrongdoing will follow, only that now mankind will not even have the consolation that the violence it must call crime is indeed characteristic of evil men only?"

In our revolutionary situation the question is just as pressing as it was in the time of the French Revolution.

B. Relation Between the Masses and the Elite

Besides the influence of the French Revolution, we find in all revolutions the question of the relation between the masses and the elite. Here we must make a sharp distinction, however, between the old elite of the establishment and the new elite who carry the ideals of the revolution. The distinction becomes clear as a feeling of discontent grows strong in both the elite and the masses.

The masses go into action only as a deep feeling of discontent is coupled with the occurrence of some significant change in national life: a defeat in war; the rise of an unbearable tyranny; the collapse of the economy or some other change that vitally affects the life of the masses. Poverty by itself does not start revolutions. Every century has seen bitter poverty. But only as change or renewal appears possible does poverty or political oppression seem unbearable. In the developing countries the contrast between the petty rich and privileged elite on one hand and the great mass of poor on the other tends to become greater. During colonial periods the elite consisted for the most part of foreigners; in Latin America, however, there now is a native elite. Moreover, the differences become clearer and more flagrant as the new elite are able to afford the luxuries of Western technological culture.

The masses, precisely because they are poor, do not quickly move into action. A general apathy is often the mark of a rural society whose subsistence is marginal. Leaders are needed to inspire the masses with a hope of change, leaders who *represent* the masses as well as speak to them. The phrase "the people" is the key to any understanding of the French Revolution. But the mass, the people, have no way to express their agreement with the ideas and goals of the leaders. In the French Revolution the destruction of the monarchy actually meant freedom only for a few. The masses, freed from the tyranny of the monarchy, were still under the oppression of their misery. It was Robespierre who, once the social revolution got going, said that from then on laws would be made in the name of the people. From this, seen from the vantage point of history, it followed as self-evident that Rousseau's "general will" had to replace the old notion of agreement. "Agreement" carried the thought of a conscious choice made after public debate of all opinions; but this was replaced by the word "will." "Will" closed the door on the processes of exchange of opinions which led to an eventual agreement. "Will," if it was to function effectively, had to be one and indivisible from the start.

"There can be only one will," demanded Robespierre; and this "will" was expressed by and through the leaders who "stood for" the masses. This is still essential in all revolutionary movements. And it is the reason (and often the pretext) for revolutionary regimes' not asking the people's ratification of their policies and decisions. The regime incarnates the will of *the people*, and this rules out the possibility of a difference of opinion.

C. Responding to the Situation

Revolutionaries have no eye for situational differences. The French revolutionaries themselves improvised for the most part, responding to the situation of the moment. Every revolution has something special about the way it develops, and this is why historians have trouble dealing with several revolutions alongside each other. It is hard to generalize and make universal rules out of them all.

But revolutionaries are not bothered by this fact. We have already seen how revolutionaries of modern times have kept the French Revolution before them as a model of how revolutions always develop. This is why they tend to overlook the large cultural differences in the countries they now consider ripe for revolution. They persist in seeing all situations in terms they borrow from the Western capitalist world. The question is whether the masses of the third world are really like the proletariat of nineteenth-century Europe. Moreover, the project of "nation building" reveals one of the huge problems of new countries; there are among them no political, administrative, and economic structures, no central institutional framework, by which to channel the wishes and movements of the masses. Besides, the real thoughts and desires of the masses are inordinately hard to measure and even harder to lead and translate into action.

In any case, the beginnings of every revolution are determined by the cultural situation of each given country (culture
here intended as the totality of the life of that country). If this
is true, it follows that the development and the results of the
revolution as well are dependent on culture.

Again, it is clear that historians and other social scientists
must work together, along with anthropologists, to get a clearer
view of the galaxy of revolutionary phenomena.

D. Planning the Movement

Revolutions are marked by a belief in man's ability to
manipulate society. Man can re-create his society and his culture in his own image according to the blueprints that he
fashions of it. This is the common conviction of revolutionaries.
Culture is, of course, man-made. But it is not made in theorists'
libraries nor even in revolutionary struggle. In the first place,
there is a great variety in the cultures that men seek to
refashion. Cultures get their own forms and styles through long
histories, and new cultures can arise only on the bedrock of
these gradually developed cultural structures. This means that
planning must be based on widely varied givens.

Apart from the variations, however, the possibilities of transforming cultures, by revolution or any other means, are
extremely limited. They are limited, in the first place, because
the network of structures within any society is fantastically
complicated, so that our insight and overview of what men
can do and of what the results of their action will be are very
limited. Secondly, a society challenges revolutionists, not as a
monolithic object to be changed, but as a galaxy of interrelated
institutions, each of which requires specific political purposes
on the part of distinct political forces. This applies to nationalist revolution; it applies trebly to international revolutionary
movements. Culture, as a human creation, requires control,
and control requires power. If one talks of social and economic
changes one is talking about power. And history shows us that
man is for the most part powerless to realize his most ambitious
ideals and goals.

E. Impatience

Revolutions are marked by intense impatience. The new must come quickly. The existent is intolerable. Adding this to a belief in power to manipulate society, impatience becomes an important ingredient in revolutionary action. People live in eager expectation and firm faith that liberation is going to bring them freedom and that change is going to rescue them from social poverty. But it must yet be proven by careful observation that establishment of freedom and rescue from poverty are ever the direct results of any revolution.

We may ask how much the impatience and expectations of revolution differ from the hopes of any longing for a millennium. Is the effort to transform society by means of revolution much different from utopian or systematic planning by social scientists? Hannah Arendt argues that the social question is never resolved by revolution. Neither the French Revolution nor Marx has offered a solution. What improvements have come were achieved by technological development.

F. The Call to Revolution

Finally, a mark of revolution is a strong sense of calling in the minds of the leaders to spread the revolution. Eugen Rosenstock-Huessy says: "The only revolutions that history can deal with are those revolutions that seek to communicate themselves to the world." This says more about the problems of historians than it does about revolutions. But the important aspect of calling is clearly suggested here. The revolutionist seeks to communicate, to spread the revolution abroad, everywhere. This applies to revolutionary theorists as much as to revolutionary actors. The typical philosophy of revolution contains this constant ingredient: revolution must be shared with the world. Here is the prophetic calling to proclaim the word and disciple the nations. In this way, revolution is a religious faith.

3

WHEN REVOLUTIONS HAPPEN

Social scientists have trouble keeping the history of revolutions in focus; but they are able to work at analyzing situations that seem revolution prone. Even in doing this they have to make comparisons between present situations and the situations from which revolutions have exploded in the past. Their method is to draw up models of past revolutionary situations which can be tested (and falsified) by comparing them with similar situations in which revolution did not break out.

It may be interesting in this connection to note a few models of revolutionary situations. While doing so, however, we must keep in mind that social analysts do not all agree on the models. Revolution is, after all, a fairly recent phenomenon. Historians and theoreticians have written many volumes about it. But while we know what individual philosophers and historians say about revolutions, we still do not have a systematic study of revolution as such. No wonder, then, that we have to sort through a confused set of social science jargon to get anywhere: the thing we want to understand is both extremely complex and quite recent.

There are incomplete models in which some of the marks of revolution that we noted in the previous chapter can be seen in their internal relationships. There are also more integrated models. The incomplete models tempt students to observe a one-sided determinism precisely because they forget that the model is incomplete—i.e., all the factors are not in.

The classic example of the incomplete model is the one fashioned by Marx. Marx's model is important because it did reveal for the first time a fundamental truth about revolution. It is partial because he let his one truth blind him to complexities that falsified his model. In any case, Marx's model is important, partly because of the truth it contains, but more because of the magnetic attraction it has on people in the developing areas of the world.

Marx, in his later period, worked on the premise of his own views of the structure of society. He saw society made up of a substructure (production techniques) and a superstructure. The superstructure was determined by the substructure. Techniques of production tend, he thought, to create definite patterns in the relationships between capital and production which in turn lead to the existence of social classes.

It is characteristic of the power structures that are created out of techniques of production that they zealously seek to maintain themselves even after the techniques of production that created them are changed. The new production techniques meanwhile tend to stimulate strong counterpowers that challenge the old ones, and the struggle between the two powers finally culminates in revolution. Herein lies the irresistible course of revolution.

The part of Marx's model that fascinates the developing countries is the notion that only the introduction of new techniques of production can bring about real progress toward total change.

H. Janne (*Un Modèle théorique du phénomène revolutionnaire*, 1962) also builds a model of revolution on the basis of the structure of society: revolution is the exchange of one structure for another. A diagram of Janne's model looks like this:

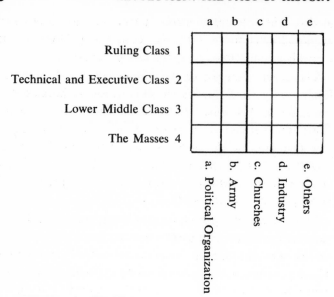

The *vertical strata* are formed by the great functional organizations of society. They exist side by side with each other. Each contains segments of the horizontal strata of society. Thus, all the vertical organizations participate in the same culture as does the whole of society, though each with different accents. And they thus have a strong integrating influence on the whole society.

The *horizontal strata* are formed out of the classic "layers" of the social hierarchy, all of which are marked by generally similar mentalities, similar interests, and similar life-styles. These horizontal layers also experience the one culture of the total society, but each in its own way. They form subcultures of the whole, and so far miss out on the integrating influence.

The diagram suggests the tensions that are inherent in the way the horizontal and vertical layers of society cross each other. Herein lies the origin of revolution. The higher layers represent the culture as a whole more fully than do the lower layers. And as the lower levels, after becoming more conscious of their situation, begin to reject their role and resist the domination of the higher levels, their subculture will define the culture of the whole. This creates a new social structure.

The more rigid the horizontal stratification, the more likely is the change to come about through revolution. Precisely what conditions must be present if the situation is to explode in revolution is left unclear by Janne. This shows that talk about structures tells us little about historical *process*.

Chalmers Johnson offers another model of the revolutionary situation (*Revolutionary Change*, 1966). He starts out with the old (obsolete?) notion that society is a functionally integrated whole, with various structures that exist in a balance of power. Whenever internal or external pressures are put on the members of a structure so that they begin to see their roles in a new way, the structure tends to malfunction. If a response made to correct the malfunction meets resistance from the elite class, the malfunction tends to spread to other structures. From this Johnson arrives at a formula: manifold malfunction + irreconcilable elite + X = revolution. X stands for the occasions that trigger the revolution—the catalysts that bring the process of conflict to the critical moment.

Here, once more, we have a theoretical model that leaves open all sorts of historical processes that need to come to life.

James C. Davies takes Marx's theory that men turn to revolution whenever their lot gets bad enough that they have "nothing to lose but their chains," and combines it with de Tocqueville's counterobservation that people come to the point of revolution only after experiencing enough improvement in their lot to convince them that poverty is no longer inevitable for them. Davies says that both help us predict revolution if they are set in the proper chronological order. A trend toward revolution requires on one hand a continuing expectation that needs will be satisfied, and on the other a threat that the needs will *not* be satisfied in spite of a preliminary taste of improvement. This theory is illustrated by the following diagram:

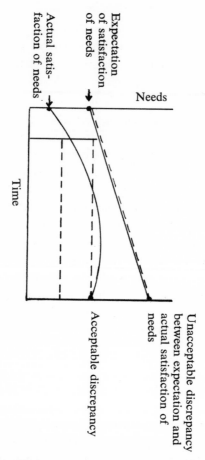

We may question whether this model was falsified by the depression years of the 1930s. It is possible that the expectation level fell along with the level of actual satisfaction of needs during that time. If this is true, the model seems to be of little help.

The various models of revolution give us little more than theoretical perspective. They point to several conditions within revolutionary situations, but they fail to tell us when such conditions actually produce revolution.

4

SOME TYPES OF REVOLUTION

Chalmers Johnson suggests several types of revolution. The Jacquerie, named after the peasant revolt of the fourteenth century toward the end of the Hundred Years' War between England and France, was really a rebellion and not a revolution. The rise of millenarianism, on the other hand, does suggest a type of revolution, and is very important for the third world. This type hopes for a general and radical transformation of the world, a world free from all its present faults, realized finally in the millennium. But the kind of revolutionary thinking typical of the French Revolution and all modern revolutions is absent in millennialism; and the modern revolution, in turn, does not typically expect the new age to come on the wings of a messianic deliverer, as does millennialism.

Then there is anarchism, which, after Bakunin, diminished in importance. It plays no role at all in the newly arisen countries.

This leaves us with the Jacobin-communist revolution, which has all of the marks mentioned previously. We need not go over these again, but we must mention the subtle, careful, and thoughtful observations that Wertheim makes about this type. Essential to the process of modernization, in many instances, according to Wertheim, is a revolutionary arousal of the organized rural proletariat. Wertheim sees a determinism at work in the historical progress of developing countries, the start of which lies in rural society. In this society the internal differences are slight. And in resistance to colonialism a nationalist ideology takes root among the people, often stimulated by the presence of a charismatic leader. This takes the form of populism. An example is Sukarno and Marhaenism, the label Sukarno gave to the proletarian movement among the rural people of Indonesia. After a while, the charismatic leader is confronted by the "efficient manager" type—the educated specialists, the bureaucrats, and especially the army. In the constellation that results, the bureaucrats and the army support the status quo and thus accentuate class tensions. The whole process finally runs its course until the "revolutionary movement of the organized rural proletariat" erupts in actual revolution. The revolution, in most cases, pushes the process of modernization a long step forward.

The last phase can be represented by the guerilla strategy of a Mao or a Castro. But the picture does not take into account the cultural differences that exist between, let us say, China, Indonesia, Africa, and Latin America. It also ignores the possibility that the bureaucracy and the army may also be stimulating factors in modernization. More important, it does not deal realistically with the personal limitations of the leader, or with influences brought to bear from foreign sources.

It is also a moot point whether class struggle will actually erupt in the third world. Nyerere of Tanzania insists that it is absent in his country. And B. Gunawan has shown that in the Indonesian coup d'etat of 1964 we had a conflict not between classes, but between communists, Moslems, and nationalists, with class war all but absent.

Johnson mentions the militarized revolt of the masses as a unique type of revolution. This type is usually a more carefully planned, more organized, more detailed form of the Jacobin-communist type of revolution. Examples of militarized revolt of the masses might be Ireland in 1916-1923, Algeria in 1954-1962, and above all China of 1937-1948. Mao plotted the mainlines of his revolution back in 1936 in a plan that finally achieved victory in 1949. It embraces five phases.

(1) The mobilization of the *long-suffering* population. The support of the masses is the one thing needful for genuine guerilla action. Mao makes this a categorical necessity, and Che Guevara confirms it in his book, *Guerrilla War* (1961).

(2) The organization of the mobilized population. The last phase of the organization is an "infra structure of rebellion," or an "autonomous government." Maoist theory requires revolutionary bases within the country, but it is possible that the military bases may lie outside the borders of the country being revolutionized, existing within so-called "privileged places of asylum."

(3) The building of a large revolutionary army around a core of party members. The army is supported by the population, which provides it with the needs to carry on its military action. To keep the support of the populace, it is essential that the army be strictly disciplined.

(4) Perfection of the most effective military tactic. This usually means guerilla warfare. Guerilla warfare is the method of fighting in units of partisans or in relatively small groups of regular troops disguised as civilians, who mingle inconspicuously among the populace.

(5) Dedication to a lengthy war. Guerilla warfare is the beginning of the end of revolution, but it is not the end. Only as victory appears certain does guerilla war give way to conventional fighting. The attack on Dien Bien Phu is a classic example of the transition.

Essentially, the strategy of a militarized revolt is directed at winning the support of the masses and serving the well-prepared political purposes of the leaders. Organized mass revolt is a kind of revolution that occurs under a leadership that knows fully what it is after.

The several types of revolution reveal a continuous line of development, in consciousness of purpose, in organization, and in direction of the movement, beginning with the wholly spontaneous and chaotic peasant revolt and ending with the militarized revolt of the masses. But what is remarkable here is that they also suggest a real historical order. The French and Russian revolutions, whose initial phases were lacking in any serious strategic planning, are types that apparently belong to the past. Future types of revolution will most likely be a combination of the Jacobin-communist and the militarized mass revolt from the beginning. In short, future revolutions will present us at their start with well-planned, organized violence.

5

VIOLENCE

Violence has been with us always. And it has not always been called evil. Violence is honored as a form of bravery in some Indian cultures, for example, as well as among some Arabian nomads, as it was also in medieval knighthood. In other cultures violence is accepted as a sacred obligation, as among the headhunters of certain old Indonesian communities. Violence was often considered necessary for the prosperity of the country and for initiation into manhood.

Other cultures, like the Zuni Indians and Bushmen, are definitely nonviolent.

European culture has always tended toward violence. The "Peace of God" which the church tried to enforce on the Middle Ages never succeeded. Jurists in the tradition of Hugo Grotius tried to place war under some definite rules in order to limit its violence. But violence directed against foreign-based tyranny, toward national independence, or on behalf of national self-determination, is almost always approved.

Had the Czechs and Slovaks been able by violence to resist the German invasion, most of us would have applauded. Violence is digestible if it is dedicated to winning or keeping freedom in the political sense. We have applauded many instances of violent revolution against colonial powers that led to the establishing of independent states. But revolution against colonialism almost always turns everything upside down and, it appears, as Frantz Fanon (*Les Damnes de la Terre,* 1961) says, violence is unavoidable and plays a positive role in it. Violence provides an outlet for primitive feelings of loyalty. A new nation is forged together in and through violence. "Whenever the masses are mobilized in a war for liberation, the thought of the common task, the national and historical unity-in-destiny is forged in the people's mind." After the struggle for liberation is won, the task of nation building begins. And violence continues to play its role in "Nation Building" in the forced liquidation of regionalism and tribalism.

This is a fairly universal experience of the decolonized lands. Fanon goes further and says that violence plays an essential role in the decolonized individuals. Violence, he claims, frees the decolonized person of his inferiority complex, of his apathy or hopelessness. This is not refuted by the postcolonial situation, though it must, as a generalization, be qualified. Countries that did not undergo violent struggle for liberation are also seeking to overcome their tribalism, and inferiority complex is being transcended in many places without the violence of a war of liberation.

The place of violence in establishing political freedom and solving social problems needs to be discussed also. The systematic use of violence was worked out by Che Guevara and Regis Debray for the guerilla strategy in Latin America. It aims at winning political power through total and violent revolution after the pattern of the militarized revolt of the masses worked out by Mao. Guevara did not develop a clear vision of future goals. Even less did he envision the processes of development toward them. All was centered on the immediate goal of political liberation.

The central question is whether violence is required, even in liberation. Does it help or hinder the quest for an order with greater social and economic justice?

As we raise the question we must keep in mind that violence is almost omnipresent now apart from revolution and that violence is advocated and used by those in power as a means of maintaining the existing order. We must also, with this in mind, make some sharp distinctions between various *kinds* of violence. The rulers of the old African kingdoms were terribly violent, even bloodthirsty; but no one denied the royal right to violence. Only when a considerable faction of the people begin to question the legitimacy of their rulers' violence, as has happened in Latin America, is this approval withdrawn. In Latin America they speak of "violencia blanca" or white violence. "Violencia blanca" gets worse as resistance to it heightens. "Violence calls forth violence" is a thesis hardly debated. But is it always true? At least it must be tested. We can at any rate just as easily contend that where "violencia blanca" is overwhelmingly effective there will be no counterviolence but rather lackluster resignation.

The old colonial situation sometimes presented still another image. Domination by the whites was often so complete and imposing that it still evokes admiration, even in Africa. Colonial mastery was seen in some parts of Indonesia as inevitable, accepted as the will of Allah. But in other parts the colonial rulers were heroically resisted. Doubt gradually took hold as time went on, and the legitimacy of colonial violence was subverted in the people's consciousness.

But the question of the effectiveness of violence, of whether it is a technique that works, must also be faced.

In South America the situation is complicated in that "violencia blanca" is practiced by an intransigent elite of Latin Americans. The elite resists the processes of development. And the army, devoted in the early nineteenth century to furthering national unity, is now seen as an instrument of what more and more people regard as illegitimate elite regimes.

Three questions must now be asked regarding what one, on a somewhat scientific basis, can expect from violent revolution.

(1) Revolution demands the sacrifice of human life. The intransigent elite is usually executed. Is it unrealistic to expect a handful of Christians to bring moderation here? Everything we know suggests rather that revolutionists accept the pattern of violence as irresistible. And until now, at any rate, the pattern has not been broken.

(2) The most important objection to revolution in our time lies in the foreign influences that, in our increasingly small world, seem unavoidably to get involved. They appear unavoidable because every revolution, no matter in what part of the world, becomes a factor in the international politics of the great powers. This only intensifies the violence and increases the victims. Spain and Vietnam are two of the most horrible examples in our time. Every new "Vietnam" means countless personal victims and terrible economic setbacks because of the enormous destruction of land and goods that foreign intervention inflicts. Besides, we must recognize that even where liberation through revolution succeeds, economic privation is likely to continue if only because foreign powers isolate the country, as has occurred with Cuba.

(3) After a revolution is finished, people expect new and better social structures to arise. But the process may well seem chaotic and anarchistic to observers on the outside. Westerners tend to take for granted a certain process of structured change similar to their own history. In the West, modernization came about as powerful central frameworks were created from which there gradually radiated out to the periphery of the people an opportunity to be included in the modernizing process. People on the periphery gradually were affected by the new control institutions and their symbols. People were integrated into the industrialization and urbanization of life before they were aroused to demand participation in the political processes. Political liberties, then, did not result in upheaval of the social structures. But in the emerging countries there is no central, institutionalized, modern industrial urban complex. The movement toward political participation goes on without an existing modern institutional framework in which the economy, the religious and intellectual life, and the administration of affairs are already integrated. The difference has an important consequence. In these lands, the new political awareness among the masses will lead to demands for which there is no political and economic framework to satisfy them. This means that the demands of the masses have no existing channels. It means therefore that a new body politic must be created that

can channel and regulate the active participation of the masses in their own destinies. In such situations, violence of some sort is almost unavoidable.

But we must nonetheless ask whether violence will help create central economic and political structures, or whether it will in fact make their creation far more difficult. The question is the more pertinent because revolution tends to liquidate whatever dominant structures still remain left over from the capitalist exploiters and the old corrupt bureaucracy.

If violence is a heavy question mark hovering over revolution, we must ask whether there are alternatives to violence.

We can assume that a will for renewal exists in most countries of the world today, a will for far-reaching, even fundamental changes in many structures of social life. Here too, we find the conviction that men *can* change things, a conviction that rests on our experience with technology and science as well as on the results of revolutionary movements since 1789.

Thought patterns tend to be stubbornly disinclined to change. Our analysis of revolutionary thought patterns attests to men's resistance to change in their ways of thinking. Thought patterns in newly developing countries are as rigid as anywhere else. They have a universal tendency toward petrification.

The French Revolution has kept a stubborn hold on revolutionary thinking as the model for revolution. But the Chinese Revolution is one that shook itself loose from the French model; it added the militarized revolt of the masses, and substituted a well-led, well-planned movement for the improvising and shifting of plans that characterized most other revolutions. Revolutionary thought in Latin America seems to be following the Chinese example.

Now the Christian communities are forced to ask themselves whether they can assimilate some or all of the modern revolutionary mind. Is it possible that today's churches in revolutionary lands face a situation parallel to that of the early church as it went out into the Greek world and assimilated much of Greek modes of thoughts? What solid ground is there for supposing that Christianity can discover something of the truth in revolutionary movements—truth, then, in the Hebrew sense of trustworthiness?

We have noted several times that liberation and freedom do not always come hand in hand. Indeed, social revolutions have yet to demonstrate that they are able to achieve both. Therefore the quest for alternatives is most urgent. We are not dealing here merely with a theoretical analysis of other people's revolutions. But we must do some criticial thinking. Perhaps we can get somewhere by considering some possibilities for alternatives to the historical pattern of revolution.

(1) Countries with unjust political structures still do accept technical progress. And if Marx was right, technology is bound to bring changes in many of the other structures of society. For example, technology changes the system of educacation. And with this, technology brings changes in the mentality and the living standards of the people. These in turn create the need for new economic and other forms of organization.

Technological progress begins, admittedly, a long-term process of change, especially where governments are corrupt or where they cooperate reluctantly. But if anything in history is inevitable—and little is—it is at least probable that growth of technological capabilities, in a world in which technology demands constant communication between countries, will bring about change wherever it occurs.

(2) Change in society entails a change of mentality, of thought patterns. The present revolutionary pattern requires indoctrination—or, to use a softer term, education—of the masses. Must education always lead to revolution? What potential does education via the media have for other means of change?

(3) What are the possibilities of passive resistance? For many, Martin Luther King's nonviolence is dead. Must it be? Or is the death of nonviolence as a viable method a myth of revolutionary dogma? What about the general strike? What about nonviolent demonstrations? Are these alternatives to violence?

(4) What are the possibilities of changing the minds of

members of the army and the police force? Is this an alternative way of stopping the "violencia blanca" in Latin America? This again is a question of how effectively nonviolent partisans can make use of the media, how effectively they can persuade, and whether reason can prevail over violence.

(5) Finally, we must mention the coup d'etat. Many coups have occurred that had nothing to do with revolution, as when one general muscles another general out of the palace. But it may be possible that a successful coup d'etat, counting on the support of most of the people, could bring sudden changes in the political and social structures in a way that would have enormous advantages over a long drawn-out revolutionary struggle. A coup d'etat at least involves a minimum of blood-letting.

94